Nick Vandome

Android Phones
for Seniors

Illustrated using Android 6.0 Marshmallow

In easy steps is an imprint of In Easy Steps Limited
16 Hamilton Terrace · Holly Walk · Leamington Spa
Warwickshire · United Kingdom · CV32 4LY
www.ineasysteps.com

Notice of Liability
Every effort has been made to ensure that this book contains accurate
and current information. However, In Easy Steps Limited and the
author shall not be liable for any loss or damage suffered by readers
as a result of any information contained herein.

Trademarks
All trademarks are acknowledged as belonging to their respective
companies.

In Easy Steps Limited supports The Forest Stewardship Council (FSC),
the leading international forest certification organization. All our titles
that are printed on Greenpeace approved FSC certified paper carry the
FSC logo.

MIX
Paper from
responsible sources
FSC® C020837

Printed and bound in the United Kingdom

ISBN 978-1-84078-775-7

Contents

1 Introducing Android Phones 7

About Android	8
About Android Phones	9
Updating Android	10
Android Overlays	11
Features of Android 7.0	12
Features of Android Phones	14
SIM Cards	16
Setting Up Your Phone	17
Android and Google	18
Creating a Google Account	20
Using a Touchscreen	22
Using Apps	24

2 Models of Android Phones 25

Samsung Phones	26
Google Phones	28
Sony Phones	29
Motorola Phones	30
HTC Phones	31
Huawei Phones	32
Lenovo Phones	33
LG Phones	34

3 Android Settings 35

Accessing Settings	36
Network Connections	37
Sound and Display	38
Personalization	39
System	40
Connect and Share	42
User and Backup	43

Applications   44
Quick Settings   45
Accessibility   47

4 Around an Android Phone   51

Viewing the Home Screen   52
Navigating Around   53
Adding Apps   54
Moving Apps   55
Working with Favorites   56
Adding Widgets   57
Changing the Background   58
Creating Folders   59
Using Notifications   60
Screen Rotation   62
Using Multiple Windows   63
Locking Your Phone   66
Searching   68
Google Assistant   71
Ok Google   73
Using Google Feeds   74

5 Calls and Contacts   79

Adding Contacts   80
Saving Contacts from Calls   82
Saving Contacts from Texts   83
From Phone to SIM   84
Editing Contacts   86
Making a Call   88
Receiving a Call   90
Setting Ringtones   93

6 Using the Keyboard   95

Keyboards with Android   96
Selecting Keyboards   97

About the Google Keyboard 98
Keyboard Settings 100
Gboard Shortcuts Bar 102
General Keyboard Shortcuts 104
Adding Text 105
Working with Text 106

7 Messaging and Email 107

Texting Contacts 108
Using a 3x4 Keyboard 110
Using Emojis 112
Adding Attachments 114
Glide Typing 115
Changing the Skin 116
Setting Up Email 118
Using Gmail 120
Going Hands-Free 122

8 Android Apps 123

Apps for Android 124
Google Apps 126
Maps 128
Notes and Memos 130
Social Media 131
Health and Fitness 132
Playing Games 133
Around the Play Store 134
Finding Apps 136
Downloading Apps 138
Uninstalling Apps 140
Updating Apps 142
App Information 144

9 Being Entertained 145

The Google Play Website 146
Music on Android 147

Downloading Music   148
Playing Music   150
Managing Music   153
Pinning Music   154
Movies and TV Shows   156
Obtaining Ebooks   158
Around an Ebook   160

10   Keeping in the Picture   161

Using Cameras   162
Adding Photos   164
Viewing Photos   166
Adding Folders   169
Editing Photos   170
Sharing Photos   172

11   Online with Chrome   173

Android Web Browsers   174
Opening Pages   175
Bookmarking Pages   176
Links and Images   178
Using Tabs   179
Being Incognito   180
Browser Settings   181

12   Staying Secure   183

Security Issues   184
About Antivirus Apps   185
Locating Your Phone   186

Index   187

1 Introducing Android Phones

Smartphones using the Android operating system are the most used phones, worldwide. This chapter gives an overview of Android on a smartphone. It also looks at creating a Google Account for use on your Android smartphone.

8   **About Android**

9   **About Android Phones**

10   **Updating Android**

11   **Android Overlays**

12   **Features of Android 7.0**

14   **Features of Android Phones**

16   **SIM Cards**

17   **Setting Up Your Phone**

18   **Android and Google**

20   **Creating a Google Account**

22   **Using a Touchscreen**

24   **Using Apps**

About Android

Android is essentially a mobile computing operating system, i.e. one for mobile devices such as smartphones and tablets.

Android is an open source operating system, which means that the source code is made available to hardware manufacturers and developers so that they can design their devices and apps in conjunction with Android. This has created a large community of Android developers, and also means that Android is not tied to one specific device; individual manufacturers can use it (as long as they meet certain specific criteria), which leads to Android being available on a variety of different devices.

Android Inc was founded in 2003, and the eponymous operating system was initially developed for mobile devices. Google quickly saw this as an opportunity to enter the smartphone and tablet market and bought Android in 2005. The first Android-powered smartphone appeared in 2008 and since then has gone from strength to strength. Android-based smartphones have a majority of the worldwide market, and it is used by numerous manufacturers on their handsets.

The main differences between the Android mobile operating system and desktop- or laptop-based ones such as Windows or macOS are:

- **No file structure**. There is no default built-in File Manager structure for storing and managing files. All content is saved within the app in which it is created.

- **Self-contained apps**. Because there is no file structure, apps are generally self-contained and do not communicate with each other, unless required.

- **Numerous Home screens**. Rather than just one Desktop, you can create numerous Home screens on an Android phone, and they can be used to store and access apps.

- **Generally, content is saved automatically as it is created**. Apps save content as it is created, so there is no Save or Save As function within many apps.

Don't forget

Android is based on the flexible and robust Linux operating system and shares many similarities with it.

About Android Phones

Android has been used on smartphones since 2008. Initially adoption was fairly slow, but this has now accelerated to the point where Android is the most widely used operating system on smartphones.

Combinations of Android phones

Since Android can be used by different manufacturers, this means that a range of the latest smartphones always run on Android. In addition, since not all older phones are designed to be upgraded to the latest version of Android, there are phones running several different versions of Android – for instance, the Google Pixel runs the latest version of Android (at the time of printing, Android 7 Nougat) while some models of older phones may still only be able to run Android 4.3 Jelly Bean. As a result, there are hundreds of combinations in terms of smartphone models and versions of Android on the market. Some are the expensive flagship models, which will run a relatively new version of Android (although not necessarily the very latest version); compared with cheaper models that can only run an older version of Android.

Checking for versions of Android

When buying an Android phone, look at the version of Android in the phone's specification. Ideally, it should be a relatively new version, in order to enable it to be upgraded to the latest version when it becomes available. Some models of Android phones reach a point where they do not have the required hardware to update to the next version of Android and are therefore stuck with the current version that they are using. This may also limit the phone's ability to download and use the latest apps that are available.

Android phone differences

Despite the variations in versions of Android, the user experience is generally the same on different Android phones. However, one area of difference is the hardware used by manufacturers. For instance, some newer Android phones have fingerprint sensors for unlocking the phone, and others have more sophisticated cameras.

Updated versions of Android are named alphabetically after items of confectionery.

Due to the range of versions of Android on smartphones, it is not feasible to cover all possibilities across different manufacturers. Therefore, this book will focus on the standard functionality of Android that is available through all versions of the operating system. It will feature Android version 6.0 Marshmallow, which is the version of Android most widely adopted on Android phones (at the time of printing). The examples will also be from a Samsung phone, the most widely used brand of smartphone on the market.

Updating Android

Since Android is open source and can be used on a variety of different devices, this can sometimes cause delays in updating the operating system on the full range of eligible Android devices. This is because it has to be tailored specifically for each different device; it is not a case of "one size fits all". This can lead to delays in the latest version being rolled out to all compatible devices. The product cycle for new versions is usually six to nine months.

Much of the general functionality of the Android operating system is the same, regardless of the version being used.

Since Android is a Google product, Google's own devices are usually the first ones to run the latest version of the software. Therefore, the Google Pixel was the first phone to run the latest version of Android, 7.0 Nougat, while others are still running previous versions, such as 4.3 Jelly Bean, 4.4 KitKat. 5.0 Lollipop or 6.0 Marshmallow. For recently-released phones, an upgrade to the latest version of Android will be scheduled into the update calendar or it might be already available to install. However, for some older Android phones the latest version of the software is not always made available. This can be because of hardware limitations, but there have also been suggestions that it is a move by hardware manufacturers designed to ensure that consumers upgrade to the latest products.

For more details about the Android settings, see Chapter Three.

The version of the Android operating system that is being used on your phone can be viewed from within the **About device** section of the **Settings** app. This is where the operating system can also be updated when a new version is available.

← About device

Android version
6.0.1

Android security patch level
February 1, 2017

Baseband version
G900FXXS1CQAV

Kernel version
3.4.0-9493471
dpi@SWDD6318 #1
Mon Feb 13 20:20:49 KST 2017

Build number
MMB29M.G900FXXS1CQBW

SE for Android status
Enforcing
SEPF_SECMOBILE_6.0.1_0030
Mon Feb 13 20:29:10 2017

Android Overlays

Because Android is an open source operating system, it means that manufacturers can amend it, to a certain extent, when they add it to their phone models. This keeps the core Android operating system, but the user interface can be adapted so that it becomes specific to each manufacturer. This is known as an "overlay" and means that the appearance of Android will be different on, for instance, a Samsung phone and a HTC one. However, the operation of Android will still be the same on different brands of phones and, in most cases, the appearance of the user interface will be very similar and still recognizable as Android.

If you are familiar with one brand of Android phone and then switch to another, it may take a little while to get used to the overlay of the new phone. However, the underlying functionality should be the same.

In addition to overlays, manufacturers can also add their own apps to their brand of Android phone and, in some cases, have their own app store for downloading more apps.

The one phone that does not have any kind of overlay is the Google Pixel: since Google own Android, they use the operating system in its purest form on their phones.

Features of Android 7.0

The latest version of Android (at the time of printing) is Android 7.0 Nougat, which is only available on a limited number of Android phones. However, much of its functionality is the same as the more widely used version of Android, 6.0 Marshmallow, although there are some enhancements, particularly for notifications:

Android 7.0 Nougat also has enhanced multi-tasking, for using two or more windows at the same time.

Quick Switch

Double-tap on the **Recent Items** button to toggle between the two most recently used apps. This is known as **Quick Switch**. Each app is shown full-screen when the button is double-tapped.

Grouped notifications

In Android 7.0 Nougat, notifications from apps are grouped together, so that you can view similar notifications at the same point in the Notification panel and action them accordingly.

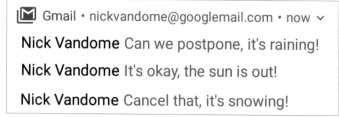

Gmail • nickvandome@googlemail.com • now ⌄

Nick Vandome Can we postpone, it's raining!

Nick Vandome It's okay, the sun is out!

Nick Vandome Cancel that, it's snowing!

Replying to notifications

Also, for some apps such as those for messaging, it is possible to reply directly to a notification without opening the specific app.

Skype • ⌃

Eilidh Vandome
Hi, how are you?

REPLY TO EILIDH VANDOME

Notifications quick settings

In Android 7.0 Nougat it is possible to apply quick notifications settings to an app directly from the Notification panel, so that you can manage how specific apps use notifications without having to go into the Settings app. To do this:

For more details about using notifications, see pages 60-61.

1 Press and hold on a notification in the Notification panel

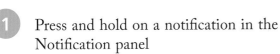

28 applications updated
AVG AntiVirus FREE for Android, Maps - Navigation & Transit,

2 Tap on one of the options for how you want notifications from the app to operate

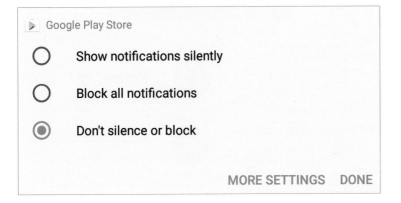

3 Tap on the **Done** button to apply the selection in Step 2, or tap on the **More Settings** button to access the notification options in the Settings app

Features of Android Phones

The button for turning a phone on and off is located on the side of the body of the device in most cases, as are the other buttons and ports that can be used for various functions on your phone.

On/Off button. This can also be used to put the phone into Sleep mode. Press and hold for a couple of seconds to turn on the phone. Press once to put it to sleep or wake it up from sleep.

Don't forget

On the Power off screen there are also options for **Airplane mode**, which turns off all network communications on the phone, and **Restart**, to turn off the phone and then turn it back on again. This can be used if the phone freezes and cannot be used normally.

Turning off. To turn off an Android phone, press and hold on the On/Off button until the **Power off** button appears on the screen. Tap on this to turn the phone off.

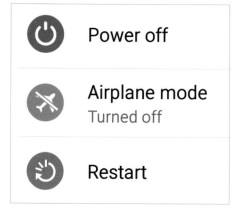

⏻	Power off
✈	Airplane mode Turned off
↺	Restart

Volume button. This is usually a single button on the opposite side to the On/Off button. Press at either end to increase or decrease volume.

Cameras. There is the main, rear-facing camera (on the back of the phone) for taking pictures. Most phones also have a front-facing camera (on the screen side of the phone), which is usually a lower resolution and is useful for making video calls or taking "selfies", as the user can view the screen at the same time as using the camera.

"Selfies" are photos taken of yourself, using the front-facing camera (on the screen of the phone).

Headphone jack. This is used to connect a headphone cable, and is usually at the top or bottom of the phone.

Micro USB port. This can be used to attach the phone to an adapter for charging the phone, or to a computer for charging or to download content from (or upload to) the phone, using the supplied USB cable. Once the phone is connected to a computer it will show up as a removable drive in the file manager, in the same way as an item such as a flashdrive.

An increasing number of phones, particularly the higher-end models, have a fingerprint sensor on the body of the phone that can be used to unlock the phone with a unique fingerprint. Fingerprint sensors have to be set up by using the applicable item (usually in the Settings app) and then pressing on the sensor several times so that it can identify your unique fingerprint. More than one fingerprint can usually be set up for use with the sensor.

microSD cards. These can be inserted into the appropriate slot on the body of the phone to increase the amount of storage for items such as photos and music.

SIM Cards

The SIM card for your Android phone will be provided by your mobile carrier, i.e. the company which provides your cellular phone and data services. Without this, you would still be able to communicate using your phone, but only via Wi-Fi and compatible services. A SIM card gives you access to a mobile network too. Some phones have a slot on the side (a SIM tray) for inserting a SIM card, while others have a slot in the back of the phone. To insert a SIM card into the latter:

Don't forget

SIM cards usually use 3G or 4G networks for providing cellular phone and data services, e.g. texting and messaging. 4G is faster, but 3G is more widely available.

Don't forget

Some Android phones, particularly newer models, have the SIM tray located around the body of the phone. The tray can be removed to insert the SIM card (a special key is needed for this, provided with the phone). If the SIM tray is accessed in this way, it is common for the battery to be non-removable.

1 Remove the back panel of the phone

2 The SIM tray is often positioned next to the battery. The battery has to be removed to gain access to the SIM tray

3 Place the SIM card into the SIM tray – line up the notch on the SIM card with the icon next to the SIM tray, so that the gold contacts are facing down and aligned with those on the phone – and push it firmly into place

4 Replace the battery, and the back panel of the phone

5 If the SIM is working properly, this symbol should appear on the top toolbar on the phone's screen, after you turn it on

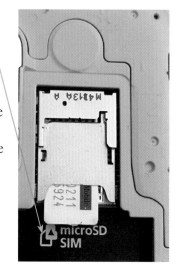

Setting Up Your Phone

When you first turn on your phone (by pressing and holding the On/Off button) you will be taken through the setup process. This only has to be done once, and some of the steps can be completed or amended at a later time, usually within the **Settings** app. Some of the elements that can be applied during the setup process are:

- **Language**. This option lets you select the language to use for your phone. Whichever language is selected will affect all of the system text on the phone, and it will also apply to all user accounts on the phone.

- **Wi-Fi**. This can be used to set up your Wi-Fi so that you can access the web and online services. In the **Select Wi-Fi** window, tap on the name of your router. Enter the password for your router and tap on the **Connect** button.

- **Google Account**. At this stage you can create a Google Account, or sign in with an existing one. Once you have done this, you will have full access to the Google Account services and you will not have to enter your login details again. (A Google Account can also be set up at a later time, see pages 20-21.)

- **Apps & data**. This option can be used to set up your new phone from a backup that you have made on another device. This will include all of the apps and settings that you have on the other device. You can also set up your phone as a new device.

- **Google services**. This includes options for which of the Google services you want to use, including backing up your phone, using location services, and sending feedback to Google.

- **Google Feeds**. This is the personal digital information and news feed that can be used to display a range of cards with the information that is most important to you (see pages 74-78).

Most routers require a password when they are accessed for the first time by a new device. This is a security measure to ensure that other people cannot gain unauthorized access to your router and Wi-Fi.

Since Android is owned by Google, much of its functionality is provided through a Google Account.

17

Android and Google

Most phones are linked to specific companies for the provision of their services and selection of apps: Apple for the iPhone, Microsoft for the Windows Phones, and Google for phones using Android, as well as the phone's manufacturer (e.g. Samsung). As with the other phones, for Android phones you must have a linked account to get the most out of your phone. This is a Google Account, and is created free of charge with a Google email address (Gmail) and a password. Once it has been created, your Google Account will give you access to a number of the built-in Android apps and also additional services such as backing up and storing your content online.

When you first set up your phone you can enter your Google Account details, or select to create a new account. You can also do this at any time by accessing one of the apps that requires access to a Google Account. These include:

- **Play Store**, for obtaining more apps.

- **Play Movies & TV**, for obtaining movies and TV shows.

- **Play Books**, for obtaining books.

- **Play Newsstand**, for displaying news stories.

When you access one of these apps you will be prompted to create a Google Account. You do not have to do so at this point, but it will give you access to the full range of Google Account services.

Other apps such as the Photos app for storing and viewing photos can be used on their own, but if a Google Account has been set up, the content will be backed up automatically.

If you already have a Gmail Account, this will also serve as your Google Account, and the login details (email address and password) can be used for both.

When you buy anything through your Google Account, such as music, apps or movies, you will have to enter your credit or debit card details (unless you are downloading a free app), which will be used for future purchases through your Google Account.

Some of the benefits of a Google Account include:

- Access from any computer or mobile device with web access, from the page **accounts.google.com/** Once you have entered your account details you can access the online Google services, including your Calendar, Gmail and the Play Store.

- Keep your content synchronized and backed up. With a Google Account, all of your linked data will be automatically synchronized so that it is available for all web-enabled devices, and it will also be backed up by the Google servers if you have set this up in Google Drive (see page 43).

If you buy items from the Play Store through your Google Account on the web, they will also be available on your Android phone.

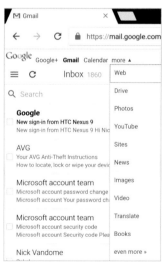

A new Google Account can also be created within **Settings** > **Accounts** on your phone. Tap on the **Add account** button and tap on the **Google** button. Then enter the required details for the new Google Account (see pages 20-21).

- Peace of mind that your content is protected. There is a **Security** section on your Google Account web page where you can apply various security settings and alerts.

Creating a Google Account

A new Google Account can be created in the following different ways:

- During the initial setup of your Android phone.

- When you first access one of the relevant apps, as explained on page 18.

- From the **Settings** app, by selecting the **Accounts > Add an account** option.

For each of the above, the process for creating the Google Account is the same:

Don't forget

During the account setup process there is also a screen for account recovery, where you can add an answer to a question so that your account details can be retrieved by Google if you forget them.

1 On the **Add your account** screen, tap on the **Or create a new account** option

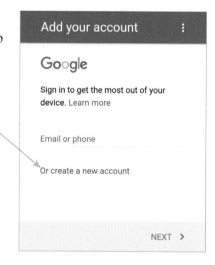

Add your account ⋮

Google

Sign in to get the most out of your **device.** Learn more

Email or phone

Or create a new account

NEXT >

2 Enter the first and last name for the new account user, then tap on the **Next** button

Create a Google Account

First name
Nick

Last name
Vandome

NEXT >

3 Enter a username (this will also become your Gmail address), then tap on the **Next** button at the bottom of the screen

How you'll sign in

You'll use this username to sign in to your Google Account

Username

nickvandome30   **@gmail.com**

Only use A-Z, a-z, and 0-9

NEXT ›

A username for a Google Account is a unique name created by the user, which is suffixed by @gmail.com.

4 Create a password for the account and then re-enter it for confirmation. Tap on the **Next** button at the bottom of the screen

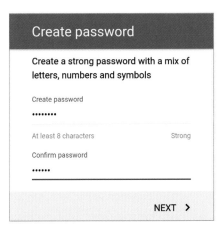

Create password

Create a strong password with a mix of letters, numbers and symbols

Create password

••••••••

At least 8 characters   Strong

Confirm password

••••••

NEXT ›

If your chosen username has already been taken, you will be prompted to amend it. This can usually be done by adding a sequence of numbers to the end of it, but make sure you remember the sequence correctly.

5 On the **Your Google Account** page, tap on the **Next** button to sign in with your new account

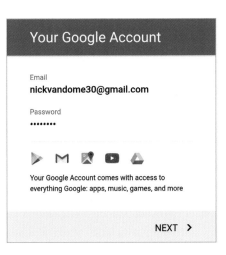

Your Google Account

Email
nickvandome30@gmail.com

Password
••••••••

Your Google Account comes with access to everything Google: apps, music, games, and more

NEXT ›

21

Using a Touchscreen

The traditional method of interacting with a computer is by using a mouse and a keyboard as the input devices. However, this has all changed with smartphones; they are much more tactile devices that are controlled by tapping and swiping on the touchscreen. This activates and controls the apps and settings on the phone, and enables you to add content with the virtual keyboard that appears at the appropriate times.

Gently does it

Touchscreens are sensitive devices and only require a light touch to activate the required command. To get the best out of your touchscreen:

Hot tip

If you are using your phone in an area where there is likely to be moisture, such as in the kitchen if you are following a recipe, cover the touchscreen in some form of light plastic wrap to protect it from any spills or splashes.

- Tap, swipe or press gently on the screen. Do not use excessive force and do not keep tapping with increasing pressure if something does not work in the way in which you expected. Instead, try performing another action and then returning to the original one.

- Tap with your fingertip rather than your fingernail. This will be more effective in terms of performing the required operation, and is better for the surface of the touchscreen.

- For the majority of touchscreen tasks, tap, press or swipe at one point on the screen. The exception to this is zooming in and out on certain items (such as web pages), which can be done by swiping outwards and pinching inwards with thumb and forefinger.

- Keep your touchscreen dry, and make sure that your fingers are also clean and free of moisture.

- Use a cover to protect the screen when not in use, particularly if you are carrying your phone in a jacket pocket or a bag.

- Use a screen cloth to keep the screen clean and free of fingerprints and smears. The touchscreen should still work if it has fingerprints and marks on it, but it will become harder to see clearly what is on the screen.

...cont'd

Touchscreen controls

Touchscreens can be controlled with three main types of actions. These are:

- **Tapping**. Tap once on an item such as an app to activate it. This can also be used for the main navigation control buttons at the bottom of the touchscreen, or for items such as checkboxes when applying settings for specific items.

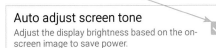

Auto adjust screen tone
Adjust the display brightness based on the on-screen image to save power.

- **Pressing**. Press and hold on an item on the Home screen to move its position or place it in the **Favorites Tray** at the bottom of the screen.

- **Swiping**. Swipe down from the top of the Home screen to access the **Notification panel** and the **Quick Settings**, and swipe left and right to view all of the available Home screens, or to scroll through photo albums.

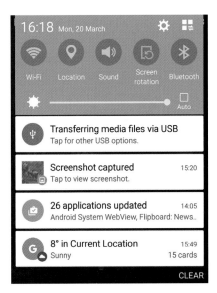

For more information about working with apps on the Home screen and the Notification panel see Chapter Four. For details about Quick Settings, see pages 45-46.

23

Using Apps

One of the great selling points for Android phones is the range of apps that are available from third-party developers. At the time of writing there are at least 2.8 million Android apps on the market. Some are free, while others are paid for.

The built-in apps are the ones that give the initial functionality to your phone, and include items such as email, web browser, calendar, calculator and maps. They appear as icons on your phone's Home screen, or in the All Apps area (see page 52), and are accessed by tapping lightly on them once.

Managing apps

When you switch from one app to another you do not have to close down the original one that you were using. Android keeps it running in the background, but in a state of hibernation so that it is not using up any memory or processing power on your phone. To do this:

Don't forget

If your phone is running low on memory it will automatically close any open apps to free up more memory. The ones that have been inactive for the longest period of time are closed first.

Don't forget

New apps for Android phones are available through the Play Store, or directly from the developer's website. They can be downloaded from there and will then appear on your phone. (See pages 134-139.)

1 Tap on an app to open it and move through its screens as required. Tap on the **Home** button on the phone's Navigation bar at the bottom of the screen to return to the Home screen at any point. The app will remain open in the background

2 Tap on the app again. It will open up at the point at which you left it

You can also move back to the Home screen by tapping on the **Back** button. This takes you back through the screens that you have accessed within the app, until you reach the app's Home screen, at which point the next screen back will be the phone's Home screen.

2 Models of Android Phones

There are a huge number of different Android phones on the market. This chapter looks at some of the leading manufacturers and a few of the phones they make.

26 **Samsung Phones**

28 **Google Phones**

29 **Sony Phones**

30 **Motorola Phones**

31 **HTC Phones**

32 **Huawei Phones**

33 **Lenovo Phones**

34 **LG Phones**

Don't forget

RAM stands for Random Access Memory, which is the memory that is used to process operations that the phone is performing. Usually, the more RAM, the better.

Hot tip

A large number of smartphones, particularly the high-end models, have the capacity for additional storage through the use of a microSD card, which fits into a slot on the side of the body of the phone. This can increase the phone's storage considerably – up to 256GB in some cases.

Samsung Phones

Samsung is the market leader in terms of the number of smartphones sold globally, partly due to the fact that it offers a considerable range of models; from its flagship Galaxy S models, to a range of cheaper models.

Samsung smartphones use the TouchWiz interface as an overlay for Android.

Some of the Samsung phones to look at include:

Galaxy S series

This includes the Galaxy S8 and S8+, which are Samsung's latest rivals to Apple's iPhone. The specifications include:

- Display: 5.8 inches (diagonally); 6.2 inches for S8+.
- Weight: 155g; 173g for S8+.
- RAM: 4GB for both.
- Memory: internal, 64GB for both.
- Operating system: Android 7.0 Nougat for both.
- Main camera: 12MP for both.
- Iris scanner for unlocking the phones.
- Fingerprint sensor for unlocking the phones.
- Battery: non-removable Li-Ion 3000mAh; 3500mAh for S8+.

Galaxy A series

This is Samsung's mid-range series of phones, and includes the Galaxy A3, Galaxy A5 and Galaxy A7 (which have increasing screen sizes). Some of the specifications for them are (for A3, A5 and A7 respectively):

- Display: 4.7 inches, 5.2 inches, 5.7 inches (diagonally).

- Weight: 138g, 157g, 186g.

- RAM: 2GB, 3GB, 3GB.

- Memory: internal, 16GB, 32GB, 32GB.

- Operating system: Android 6.0.1 Marshmallow, for all.

- Main camera: 13MP, 16MP, 16MP.

- Fingerprint sensor for unlocking the phone, for all.

- Battery: non-removable Li-Ion 2350mAh, 3000mAh, 3600mAh.

Generally, higher specification models of smartphones, i.e. the most powerful and expensive, come with the latest version of Android, or can upgrade to it. Other models may be limited in terms of the version of Android that they can run.

Galaxy J series

This is Samsung's range of budget smartphones, and includes the Galaxy J1, Galaxy J5 and Galaxy J7 (which have increasing screen sizes). Some of the specifications for them are (for the J1, J5 and J7 respectively):

- Display: 4.5 inches, 5.2 inches, 5.5 inches (diagonally).

- Weight: 131g, 159g, 170g.

- RAM: 1GB, 2GB, 2GB.

- Memory: internal, 8GB, 16GB, 16GB.

- Operating system: Android 5.1.1 Lollipop, Android 6.0.1 Marshmallow, Android 6.0.1 Marshmallow.

- Main camera: 5MP, 13MP, 13MP.

- Battery: removable Li-Ion 2050mAh, 3100mAh, 3300mAh.

The phones listed in this chapter are just a small number of the hundreds of Android models that are on the market, covering different specifications and different versions of the Android operating system.

Google Phones

Since Android is owned by Google, it makes sense for them to have their own Android phone. This is the Google Pixel phone, which is the successor to the Google Nexus phone. It comes in the standard model or in the XL model.

The Pixel is a high-specification smartphone and, unlike the majority of Android phones on the market, comes with the latest version of Android (7.1 Nougat at the time of printing). Also, the Google Pixel will be the first phone that can update to the next version of Android when it is released.

Android on the Google Pixel is the purest form of the operating system, since unlike other manufacturers who use Android on their phones, there is no overlay on top of the standard operating system.

The Google Pixel and Pixel XL

Some of the specifications of the Google Pixel and Pixel XL are:

The Google Pixel does not have a microSD card slot for additional memory, but has unlimited cloud storage for photos.

- Display: 5.0 inches (diagonally); 5.5 inches for the XL.

- Weight: 143g; 168g.

- RAM: 4GB.

- Memory: internal, 32; 128GB.

- Operating system: Android 7.1 Nougat.

- Main camera: 12.3MP.

- Fingerprint sensor (on the back of the phone) for unlocking the phone.

- Battery: non-removable Li-Ion 2700mAh; 3450mAh.

Sony Phones

Sony is another major player in the smartphone market, and has a reputation for producing phones with particularly good cameras.

Xperia XZ

The Xperia series is the main range of Sony smartphones, with the Xperia XZ being the flagship model. Some of its specifications are (XZs model):

- Display: 5.2 inches (diagonally).

- Weight: 161g.

- RAM: 4GB.

- Memory: internal, 32GB.

- Operating system: Android 7.1 Nougat.

- Main camera: 19MP, with touch autofocus.

- Fingerprint sensor for unlocking the phone.

- Battery: non-removable Li-Ion 2900mAh.

Other Sony smartphones to look at include: the Xperia XZ Premium, the Xperia XA1, the Xperia X, and the Xperia E5.

Motorola Phones

Motorola smartphones are produced by Motorola Mobility, a company that was spun out of the original Motorola. Motorola Mobility was acquired by Google in 2011, and it was then subsequently sold to the Chinese firm Lenovo in 2014. In 2016 Lenovo announced that the Motorola smartphones would use the Moto branding.

Moto G5 Plus
The flagship Moto smartphone is the G5 Plus, and some of its specifications include:

- Display: 5.2 inches (diagonally).

- Weight: 155g.

- RAM: 3GB.

- Memory: internal, 32/64GB.

- Operating system: Android 7.0 Nougat.

- Main camera: 12MP.

- Fingerprint sensor for unlocking the phone.

- Battery: non-removable Li-Ion 3000mAh.

Don't forget

Other Motorola smartphones to look at include: the Moto M, the Moto E3, the Moto Z, and the Moto G4.

HTC Phones

HTC is a Taiwanese company that was at the forefront of the development of smartphones using the Android operating system. Despite an up and down performance in the smartphone market, HTC has produced a successful range of phones – the HTC One range, which remains a popular model.

The HTC One uses an Android overlay called Freestyle Layout, which uses a grid onto which the user can drag icons, widgets and stickers to create a customized display.

HTC One

The specifications for the HTC One include:

- Display: 5.2 inches (diagonally).

- Weight: 161g.

- RAM: 4GB.

- Memory: internal, 32/64GB.

- Operating system: Android 6.0 Marshmallow (upgradable to 7.0 Nougat).

- Main camera: 12MP, with laser autofocus.

- Fingerprint sensor for unlocking the phone.

- Battery: non-removable Li-Ion 3000mAh.

Don't forget

Other HTC smartphones to look at include: the U Ultra, the U Play, the Desire 10 and the One A9s.

Huawei Phones

Huawei is a major Chinese technology company that produces a wide range of communications devices including smartphones. Most Huawei phones which use Android also use the Emotion User Interface (EMUI) overlay.

P10 series

The latest flagship range of Huawei phones is the P10 (with additional models, the P10 Plus and the P10 Lite), and some of its specifications include:

- Display: 5.1 inches (diagonally).

- Weight: 145g.

- RAM: 4GB.

- Memory: internal, 32/64GB.

- Operating system: Android 7.0 Nougat.

- Main camera: Dual 20MP + 12MP.

- Fingerprint sensor for unlocking the phone.

- Battery: non-removable Li-Ion 3200mAh.

Don't forget

Other Huawei smartphones to look at include: the Honor 8 Pro, the Honor Magic, the Enjoy 6s, and the Mate 9.

Lenovo Phones

Lenovo is another large Chinese technology company that produces personal computers, laptops, tablets and smartphones, alongside a wide range of other devices.

Lenovo Phab series

The flagship range of Lenovo smartphones is the Phab series. Some of the specifications of the Phab Pro 2 are:

- Display: 6.4 inches (diagonally).

- Weight: 259g.

- RAM: 4GB.

- Memory: internal, 64GB.

- Operating system: Android 6.0 Marshmallow.

- Main camera: 16MP.

- Fingerprint sensor for unlocking the phone.

- Battery: non-removable Li-Ion 4050mAh.

LG Phones

LG Corporation (formerly Lucky-GoldStar Corporation) is a South Korean multinational that produces a wide range of products, from washing powder and toothpaste, to electronic devices. LG Corporation has produced a range of smartphones over the years, with particular success in the US.

G series

The flagship LG smartphone range is the G series, with one of the most recent models being the G6. Some of its specifications include:

- Display: 5.7 inches (diagonally).

- Weight: 163g.

- RAM: 4GB.

- Memory: internal, 32/64GB.

- Operating system: Android 7.0 Nougat.

- Main camera: 13MP.

- Fingerprint sensor (on the back of the phone) for unlocking the phone.

- Battery: removable Li-Po 3300mAh.

Don't forget

Other LG smartphones to look at include: the G5, the V20, and the K series of budget smartphones.

3 Android Settings

As with all computers and mobile devices, Android phones have a range of settings that can be applied to specify the operation of the device and also its look and feel.

36 Accessing Settings

37 Network Connections

38 Sound and Display

39 Personalization

40 System

42 Connect and Share

43 User and Backup

44 Applications

45 Quick Settings

47 Accessibility

Accessing Settings

We all like to think of ourselves as individuals, and this extends to the appearance and operation of our electronic gadgets. An Android phone offers a range of settings so that you can set it up exactly the way that you want, and give it your own look and feel. These are available from the **Settings** app.

To access the **Settings** app on your Android phone:

Hot tip

The Settings app can be added to the Home screen, or the Favorites Tray (see page 52), by pressing and holding on it in the All Apps section and then dragging it to the required location.

1   Tap on the **All Apps** button (see page 52)

2   Tap on the **Settings** app

3   The full range of settings is displayed. If a section is hidden, tap on a down-pointing arrow to expand the section

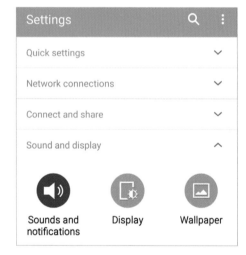

Hot tip

The Settings can also be accessed by swiping down from the top of the phone to access the Quick Settings. From here, tap on the **Settings** button at the top of the screen.

4   Tap on an item to view all of the options for it. (If necessary, tap on the options at the next level down to see their own options.) Most options will have an On/Off button, a radio button or a checkbox to tap on or off

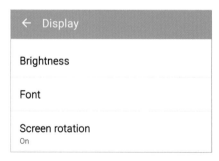

Network Connections

These settings can include:

- **Wi-Fi**. Used for turning Wi-Fi on and off on your phone, and connecting to a router.

- **Download booster**. This can be used to download large files (although this should be done using Wi-Fi rather than a cellular connection, e.g. 3G or 4G).

- **Bluetooth**. Used for connecting wirelessly to other Bluetooth-enabled devices over short distances. Both devices have to be 'paired', i.e. connected together, so that they can share content.

- **Tethering and Mobile**. This can be used to set up your phone as mobile hot-spot, so that other devices can connect to it via Wi-Fi, and then connect to the internet.

- **Airplane mode**. Check this on when taking a flight, to disable any mobile communications to or from your phone.

- **Data usage**. Used to view how much data you have downloaded and which apps are using the most data.

- **Location**. This can be used to view which apps have requested access to your location, or to turn on GPS.

- **More networks**. This can be used to access other networks such as other mobile ones, or to set up a Virtual Private Network (VPN).

The Wi-Fi setting can be used to connect to Wi-Fi in your own home and also to any public Wi-Fi hotspots. For both, you will need to use the password to access the router.

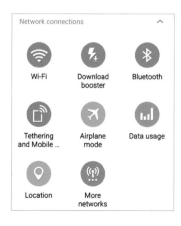

Hot tip

It is worth exploring the sound settings in some detail, as this is where you can turn on and off a lot of the system sounds, e.g. for when notifications and messages are received, keyboard sounds when you are typing, and for the Lock screen. There is also an option for haptic feedback, which creates a small vibration when pressing certain items.

Sound and Display

These settings can include:

● **Sounds and notifications**. This can be used to turn on or off the sounds for a range of functions including calls and texts, the keyboard, the touchscreen, and the Lock screen. It can be used to specify the operation of notifications on your phone.

● **Display**. Used to set the screen brightness, screen rotation and screen timeout.

● **Wallpaper**. Used to select a wallpaper for the Home screen and the Lock screen.

● **Lock screen**. Used to set a screen lock method for locking your phone.

● **Multi window**. If a phone has multi window functionality, this setting manages this option.

● **Notification panel**. This can be used to specify the items that appear in the Notification panel and the Quick Settings area.

● **Toolbox**. On some Android phones, this can be used to quickly access favorite apps.

● **One-handed operation**. On some Android phones, this can be used to control the phone's screen to make it easier to access items with one hand.

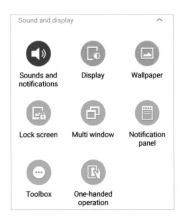

Personalization

These settings can include:

- **Easy mode**. This can be used to select a simplified version of the Home screen, and you can also select which apps appear on the Home screen.

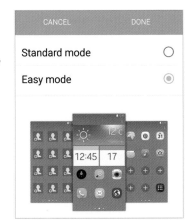

- **Accessibility**. This contains a range of accessibility settings, to make the phone easier to use for people with vision, hearing and dexterity issues.

For more details about some of the accessibility features see pages 47-50.

- **Private mode**. This can be used to hide personal content to keep it secure on your phone. This can be applied to content in specific apps.

- **Finger Scanner**. On Android phones that have a fingerprint sensor for unlocking the phone, this setting can be used to set up the sensor and register your unique fingerprint for unlocking the phone.

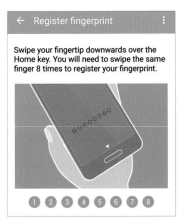

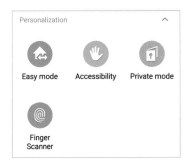

System

These settings can include:

- **Language and input**. This can be used to select a language for the items displayed on the phone and also for the keyboard. Different keyboards can also be selected here, as can options for using speech input.

- **Date and time**. Used to set your phone's date and time, either automatically or manually.

- **Safety assistance**. This can be used to enable emergency calls to be made directly from the Lock screen (even if the phone remains locked). To enable this, one person's details have to be entered as the primary contact, and they will be used in the case of an emergency.

- **Accessories**. This can be used to specify options for external devices that are connected to the phone, such as headphones, and the audio options.

- **Battery**. This displays details about your phone's battery, including how much charge is left. It also has options for optimizing battery use by putting apps that have not been used for three days or more into hibernation so that they save power. (The apps will wake up again as soon as they are selected.)

To save battery power, turn off options including Wi-Fi and Bluetooth when they are not being used, and turn the screen brightness down.

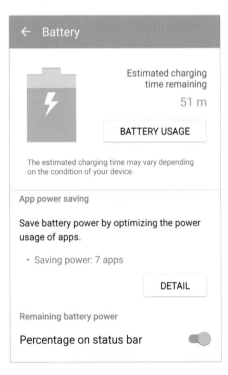

← Battery

Estimated charging time remaining

51 m

BATTERY USAGE

The estimated charging time may vary depending on the condition of your device.

App power saving

Save battery power by optimizing the power usage of apps.

· Saving power: 7 apps

DETAIL

Remaining battery power

Percentage on status bar

- **Power saving**. This setting can also be used to access power saving options, including the accessing of background data.

- **Storage**. This can be used to view the amount of storage that is available on your phone and how much has already been used up.

  Internal storage

  ← Internal storage

  8.99 GB
  Used out of 16.00 GB

  Total space
  16.00 GB

  Available space
  7.01 GB

  System memory
  4.16 GB

- **Security**. This can be used to apply encryption to the data on your phone, to make it more secure. In some cases there is also a setting for locating a lost device, via an external website.

- **Help**. Depending on the make and model of Android phone, this will contain general help options, specific to it.

- **Developer options**. This is an advanced setting that can be used by software developers who want to test newly developed apps on the phone.

- **About device**. This displays details about your phone, including options for software updates to the Android operating system, the name and model of the phone, and also the version of Android that is currently being used.

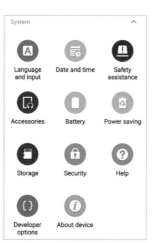

Hot tip

If there is an update available for your Android operating system, the Settings icon will have a red tag on it with a number corresponding to the number of updates available.

41

Connect and Share

These settings can include:

- **NFC**. This can be used for Near Field Communication (NFC), whereby data can be exchanged between two devices by just touching them together. Both devices must have NFC turned on, and it works best between two Android devices.

- **Nearby devices**. This can be used to give other devices access to some of the content on your Android phone. Nearby devices will recognize your phone once this has been turned on and will ask for access, usually via Wi-Fi. It is possible to select the type of content you want to share (videos, photos and music), and select the devices that you want to give access to.

- **Printing**. This can be used to download apps to enable printing from your phone. These are usually from the device manufacturer, so that the printing plugin is compatible with the phone.

- **Screen Mirroring**. This can be used to share your phone's screen with a compatible device, e.g. a high-definition TV, for watching the content on your phone on a larger screen.

- **MirrorLink**. This can be used to connect to a compatible system in a car, so that the phone can be used hands-free. The connection is usually done with a USB cable.

Beware

In order to be able to print from your Android phone you will need a wireless printer and a printing app that is compatible with your phone and the printer. Check the website of the phone's manufacturer to see if there is a list of compatible printers.

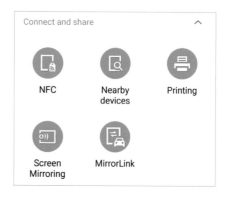

User and Backup

These settings can include:

- **Accounts**. This can be used to display the accounts that you have added to your phone, and also add new ones. This should include your Google Account, any other accounts such as webmail accounts, and social media accounts such as Twitter and Facebook.

- **Google**. This displays settings for using your Google Account, including account details and available Google services.

- **Cloud**. This can be used to connect to an online service in order to back up and sync the content on your phone. Individual phone manufacturers will usually have their own cloud services which can be used, and there is also the option to use online services such as Dropbox.

- **Backup and reset**. This can be used to back up the data on your phone to your online Google Account, and it can also be used to return the phone to its original factory settings.

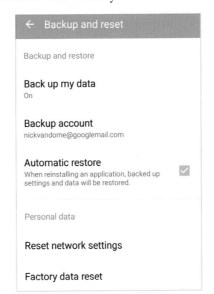

If you return your phone to its factory settings, all of the data and files on it will be lost. Therefore it is important to back it up to your Google Account or another cloud service first.

To set the backup for data on your phone, tap on the Back up my data button in the Backup and reset section. Drag the Back up my data button to On, to automatically have your device and app data backed up to Google Drive, within your online Google Account.

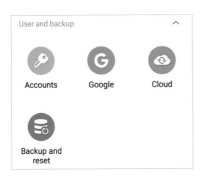

Applications

These settings can include:

- **Application manager**. This can be used to apply system settings to specific apps on the phone (this is different from the apps' own settings, which can be accessed below). Tap on an app to disable it, Force Stop it or view its data usage and permissions.

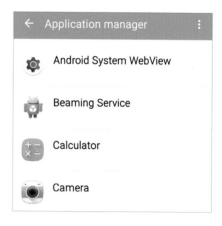

- **Default applications**. This can be used to set default apps for specific tasks, e.g. for web browsing, making calls or sending messages.

- **Application settings**. These can be used to apply settings for specific apps, usually the built-in ones. Tap on an app to view its settings and apply them accordingly, e.g. for the Contacts app.

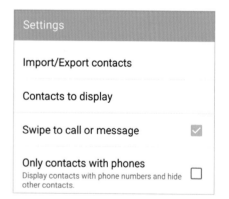

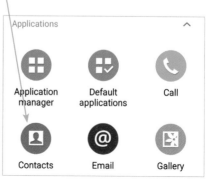

Don't forget

In some cases, the default applications will be linked to the phone's manufacturer, i.e. Samsung phones may use Samsung apps as the default for opening content such as web pages, music and videos.

Quick Settings

The full range of Android settings can be accessed from the Settings app. However, on some Android phones, there is a Quick Settings option that can be accessed from the top of the screen. To use this:

1 Swipe down from the top of the screen to access the **Quick Settings**

2 Swipe from right to left to view the other available Quick Settings options

3 Tap on this button to view the full range of Quick Settings that are available, or drag the screen downwards to extend it

4 Tap on a Quick Setting to make it active. Tap on this button to minimize the full list of Quick Settings

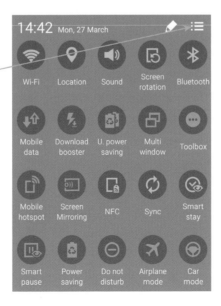

Don't forget

The Quick Settings buttons only turn the setting on or off. To access the options for a setting, tap on the **Settings** button at the top of the window.

...cont'd

Editing Quick Settings

It is possible to edit the items that appear on the Quick Settings bar. To do this:

1 Tap on the **Edit** button at the top of the window in Step 4 on the previous page

46

2 The Notification panel is opened. The items at the top are currently available in the Quick Settings; the ones below are not

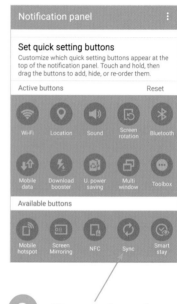

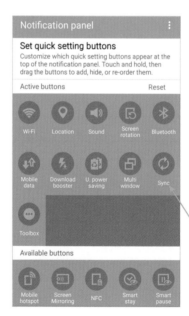

3 Drag an item from the bottom panel to include it in the Quick Settings panel (and vice versa to remove it)

4 The item is then available when the Quick Settings panel is accessed

Accessibility

It is important for phones to be accessible to as wide a range of users as possible, including those with visual or physical and motor issues. In Android this is done through the **Accessibility** settings. To use these:

1 Tap on the **Settings** app

2 Tap on the **Accessibility** button under **Personalization**

3 The main categories are listed at the top of the window. These are **Vision**, **Hearing**, and **Dexterity and interaction**. Tap on one to view the full range of settings within it

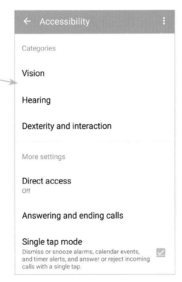

The Vision section has a **Font size** option where the font size can be increased, or decreased, for compatible apps, display and system settings.

Once an item has been selected in Step 3, double-tap on it to activate its functionality.

Vision settings

1 Tap on the **Vision** button in Step 3 and tap on the **TalkBack** button. Drag the **TalkBack** button to **On**
to activate TalkBack, whereby the phone will provide spoken information about items on screen and those which are being accessed

To turn off TalkBack, tap on the **TalkBack** button once in Step 1 and then double-tap on it to turn it off.

...cont'd

2 TalkBack also provides an **Explore by Touch** function that enhances TalkBack by providing an audio description of what is on the screen. Tap on the **OK** button to activate TalkBack

Use TalkBack?

TalkBack wants permission to:

- **Monitor your actions**
  Receive notifications when you're interacting with an app.

- **Retrieve window content**
  Inspect the content of a window you're interacting with.

- **Turn on Explore by Touch**
  Touched items will be spoken aloud and the screen can be explored using gestures.

- **Turn on enhanced web accessibility**
  Scripts may be installed to make app content more accessible.

- **Observe text you type**
  This includes personal data such as credit card numbers and passwords.

CANCEL   OK

3 The active items are highlighted by a blue outline. Tap on an item to hear an audio description

SETTINGS

4 Tap on **Magnification gestures** in the Vision section to access the setting for zooming on the screen by triple-tapping on it

 ← Magnification gestures

When this feature is on, you can zoom in and out by triple tapping the screen.

While zoomed in, you can
- Pan: Drag two or more fingers across the screen.
- Adjust the zoom level: Pinch two or more fingers together or spread them apart.

You can also temporarily magnify what is under your finger by triple tapping and holding. In this magnified state, you can drag your finger to explore different parts of the screen. Lift your finger to return to the previous state.

Note: Triple tap for magnification works everywhere except the keyboard.

When this feature is on, the response time could be slowed down in Phone, Calculator and other apps.

5 Drag this button **On** and triple-tap on the screen to zoom in on what is being viewed

Hearing settings

To use some of the Hearing settings:

1 Tap on the **Hearing** option in Step 3 on page 47

2 Tap on the **Flash notification** option to enable the screen to flash for notifications and calls

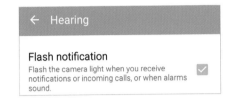

3 Tap on the **Turn off all sounds** option to mute sounds for everything

4 Tap on the **Google subtitles** button (Closed Captions)

5 Drag the **Google subtitles** button to **On** to display subtitles in compatible apps, e.g. for movies or TV shows. Select the options for how the subtitles are displayed

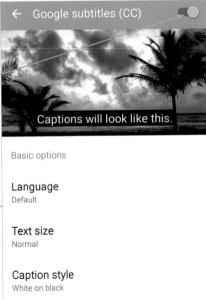

Beware

Only some apps support subtitles, so even if they are turned on they may not appear. Check in an app's specifications in the Play Store (see pages 134-135) to see if it supports subtitles.

...cont'd

Regardless of the Sound balance, keep the overall volume on your phone to a reasonable and comfortable level; if it is too loud it may cause long-term damage, particularly when using headphones.

6 Tap on the **Sound balance** option

Sound balance
Adjust the sound balance in media players for when earphones are connected.

7 Drag the slider to specify the direction of sound when using headphones

Sound balance

Left   Right
⎯⎯⎯⎯⎯⎯⎯⎯⎯⎯○⎯⎯⎯⎯⎯⎯⎯⎯⎯⎯

                          CANCEL   OK

8 Tap on the **Mono audio** checkbox to use mono if using one headphone

Mono audio
Switch audio from stereo to mono for when you are using one earphone.   ☑

Dexterity and interaction settings

To use some of the Dexterity and interaction settings:

1 Tap on the **Dexterity and interaction** option in Step 3 on page 47

2 Tap on the **Assistant menu** option to create quick access to items

3 Tap on the **Press and hold delay** option to specify a time period before a key becomes active after pressing and holding it

4 Tap on the **Interaction control** option to specify areas of the screen that can be inactive to touch

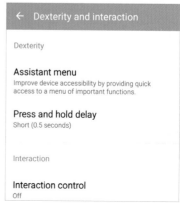

← Dexterity and interaction

Dexterity

Assistant menu
Improve device accessibility by providing quick access to a menu of important functions.

Press and hold delay
Short (0.5 seconds)

Interaction

Interaction control
Off

4 Around an Android Phone

This chapter details the Android interface and shows how to find your way around the Home screen, add apps and widgets, change the background, and lock your phone. It also covers the sophisticated range of search options that are available, including the digital voice assistant, Google Assistant, which can respond to a wide range of spoken queries.

52 **Viewing the Home Screen**

53 **Navigating Around**

54 **Adding Apps**

55 **Moving Apps**

56 **Working with Favorites**

57 **Adding Widgets**

58 **Changing the Background**

59 **Creating Folders**

60 **Using Notifications**

62 **Screen Rotation**

63 **Using Multiple Windows**

66 **Locking Your Phone**

68 **Searching**

71 **Google Assistant**

73 **Ok Google**

74 **Using Google Feeds**

Viewing the Home Screen

Once you have set up your phone, the first screen that you see will be the Home screen. This is also where you will return to when you tap the Home button (see next page). The elements of the Home screen include:

Swipe down from the Notifications bar to view the current notifications, alongside the Quick Settings (see page 45).

Hot tip

Notifications Bar

Google Search box

Home screen area. This is where the majority of your commonly-used apps and widgets will be located

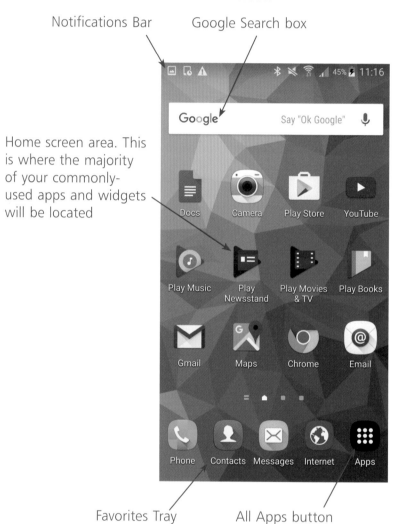

Favorites Tray

All Apps button

On different models of Android phones, the All Apps button may be located in a slightly different position. The appearance of the Home screen may also be slightly different, depending on which apps the manufacturer has chosen to appear on the Home screen and the type of overlay used.

Navigating Around

At the bottom of the Home screen there are three buttons that can be used to navigate around your phone. On some phones these are on the screen, and on others they are on the body of the phone itself.

The Navigation buttons are:

Back. Tap on this button to go back to the most recently-visited page or screen.

Home. Tap on this button to go back to the most recently-viewed Home screen at any point.

Recent Items. Tap on this to view the apps that you have used most recently. Tap on one of the apps to access it again. Swipe an app to the right to close the app, or tap on the cross in the top right-hand corner of the app.

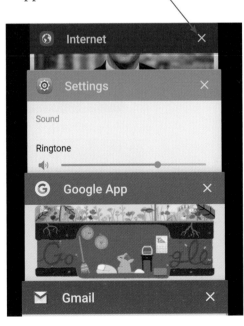

Don't forget

Most Android phones have several Home screens. Swipe left and right to move between them.

53

Hot tip

When the keyboard is being used, the **Back** button can also be used to hide the keyboard.

Adding Apps

The Home screen is where you can add and manage your apps. To do this:

1 Tap on the **All Apps** button

2 All of the built-in apps are displayed. Tap on an app to open it

3 To add an app to the Home screen, press and hold on it

4 Drag it onto the Home screen on which you want it to appear and release it

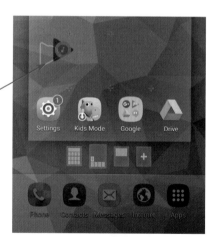

5 The app is added to the Home screen

6 Swipe left and right to move between the available Home screens

Don't forget

There are thousands more apps available for download from the Play Store. Tap on this button on the Home screen to access the Play Store (see pages 134-138).

Play Store

Don't forget

Apps can be removed from a Home screen by pressing and holding on them, and then dragging them to the top of the screen, where a **Remove** button will appear. Drag the app over the **Remove** button. This only removes it from the Home screen, not your phone. It will still be available from the All Apps section.

Moving Apps

Once apps have been added to the Home screen they can be repositioned and moved to other Home screens. To do this:

1 Press and hold on an app to move it. Drag it into its new position. A light outline appears, indicating where the app will be positioned

Apps can be moved to the left or right onto new Home screens.

2 Release the app to drop it into its new position

3 To move an app between Home screens, drag it to the edge of the Home screen

Make sure that the app is fully at the edge of the Home screen, otherwise it will not move to the next one. A thin, light border should appear just before it moves to the next Home screen.

4 As the app reaches the edge of the Home screen it will automatically move to the next one. Add it to the new Home screen in the same way as in Step 2

Don't forget

For some phones, the Favorites Tray appears along the bottom of the screen in landscape mode; for others, it appears down the right-hand side of the screen.

Hot tip

Apps can appear in the **Favorites Tray** and also on individual Home screens, but they have to be added there each time from within the **All Apps** section.

Working with Favorites

The Favorites Tray at the bottom of the Home screen can be used to access the apps you use most frequently. This appears on all of the Home screens. Apps can be added to or removed from the Favorites Tray, as required.

1 The apps in the **Favorites Tray** are visible at the bottom of the screen on all Home screens

2 Press and hold on an app in the **Favorites Tray** and drag it onto the Home screen to remove it from the Favorites Tray

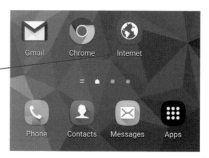

3 Press and hold on an app on the Home screen, and drag it onto a space in the **Favorites Tray** to add it there

4 The **Favorites Tray** has a limit to the number of apps that it can contain (usually four, plus the All Apps button), and if you try to add more than this, the app will spring back to its original location

Adding Widgets

Android widgets are similar to apps, except that they generally display specific content or real-time information. For instance, a photo gallery widget can be used to display photos directly on a Home screen, or a traffic widget can display updated information about traveling conditions. Widgets can be added from any Home screen:

From the screen in Step 1 you can also access Wallpapers (see page 58) and Home screen settings (for moving between Home screens).

1 Press and hold on an empty area on any Home screen and tap on the **Widgets** button

2 Swipe up and down, or sometimes left and right, to view all of the available widgets

Widget icons on the Home screens usually appear larger than those for standard apps.

3 Press and hold on a widget and drop it onto a Home screen as required, in the same way as for adding apps

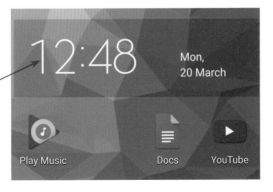

57

Changing the Background

The background (wallpaper) for all of the Home screens on your phone can be changed within the **Settings** app (**Settings** > **Wallpaper**). However, it can also be changed directly from any Home screen. To do this:

1 Press and hold on an empty area on any Home screen and tap on the **Wallpapers** button

2 Tap on one of the options from where you would like to select the background wallpaper

Hot tip

Wallpaper apps can be downloaded from the Play Store, to add a wider range of backgrounds to your phone. Enter '**wallpaper**' into the Search box of the **Apps** section of the Play Store.

3 Select a background and tap on the **Set As Wallpaper** button

4 Select whether the background is for the Home screen, the Lock screen, or both

Home screen

Lock screen

Home and lock screen

5 The selected background is applied to all Home screens

Creating Folders

As you start to use your Android phone for more activities, you will probably acquire more and more apps. These will generally be for a range of tasks covering areas such as productivity, communications, music, photos, and so on. Initially it may be easy to manage and access these apps, but as the number of them increases, it may become harder to keep track of them all.

One way in which you can manage your apps is to create folders for apps covering similar subjects, e.g. one for productivity apps, one for entertainment apps, etc. To create folders for different apps:

Don't forget

To remove an app from a folder, press and hold on it and drag it out of the folder onto a Home screen.

1 Press and hold on an app and drag it over the **Create folder** button at the top of the screen

2 A folder is created, and the app is added to the folder. Tap here to give the folder a name

3 Enter the name, and tap on the **+** button to add more items to the folder

Hot tip

Adding folders to the Favorites Tray is a good way to make a larger number of apps available here, rather than the standard four permitted.

4 Tap on the required items to select them for adding to the folder, then tap on the **Done** button

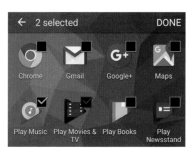

Using Notifications

Android phones have numerous ways of keeping you informed; from new emails and calendar events, to the latest information about apps that have been downloaded and installed. To make it easier to view these items, they are grouped together in the Notification panel. This appears on the Lock screen and can also be accessed from any Home screen by swiping down from the Notifications bar.

Hot tip

Settings for the Notification panel can be applied in **Settings** > **Sound and display** > **Sounds and notifications**. These can be used to specify what is shown when the phone is locked and to select notifications for specific apps (see page 38).

60

Don't forget

Tap on the **Clear** button to clear all of the current notifications. If you clear the notifications it does not delete the items; they remain within their relevant apps and can be viewed there.

1 By default, some notifications are shown on the Lock screen. Tap on a notification here to access it directly (you must unlock your phone first – see pages 66-67)

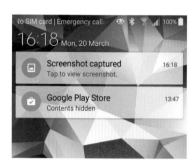

2 On any Home screen or the All Apps screen, notifications are indicated on the Notifications bar

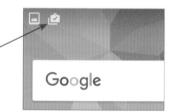

3 Swipe down from the top of any screen to access your notifications. Some of these may display more details than on the Lock screen

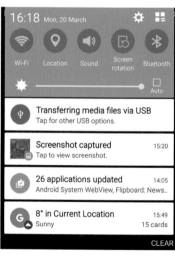

4 Tap on a notification to view its full details within the relevant app, e.g. a Gmail notification will open Gmail to view new emails

Settings for notifications

To specify which apps can display notifications and how they operate:

1 Within the **Settings** app, tap on the **Sounds and notifications** button under **Sound and display**

Sounds and notifications

2 Swipe down to the **Notification** section and tap on the **Application notifications** option

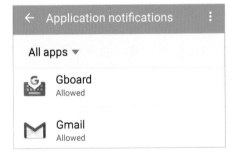

Notification

Do not disturb

Notifications on lock screen
Hide content

Application notifications

Tap on the **Do not disturb** option in Step 2 to mute your phone for all calls and notifications, apart from any exceptions that you specify.

3 Tap on the app for which you want to set notifications

← Application notifications ⋮

All apps ▾

G Gboard
   Allowed

M Gmail
   Allowed

Hot tip

Tap on the **Notifications on lock screen** option in Step 2 to select whether to **Show** or **Hide** notifications on the Lock screen.

4 Drag the **Allow notifications** button to **On** to enable notifications to be displayed for the selected app

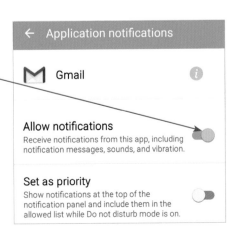

← Application notifications

M Gmail   ⓘ

Allow notifications
Receive notifications from this app, including
notification messages, sounds, and vibration.

Set as priority
Show notifications at the top of the
notification panel and include them in the
allowed list while Do not disturb mode is on.

Screen Rotation

By default, the content on a phone's screen rotates as you rotate the device. This means that the content can be viewed in portrait or landscape mode, depending on what is being used, e.g. for movies it may be preferable to have it in landscape mode, while for reading it may be better in portrait mode:

It is also possible to lock the screen so that it does not rotate when you move it. This can be useful if you are using it for a specific task and do not want to be distracted by the screen rotating if you move your hand slightly. To lock and unlock the screen rotation:

1 Drag down from the top of the screen to access the **Quick Settings** (see pages 45-46)

2 Tap on the **Screen rotation** button to enable screen rotation

3 Tap on the **Screen rotation** button again so that it is grayed-out, to disable screen rotation

Using Multiple Windows

A useful feature on some Android phones (usually running Marshmallow 6.0 or later) is the ability to view two windows at the same time. Content in each window can be worked on independently from each other. On some Android phones, Multi window view is enabled automatically; on others it has to be applied within the Settings app:

1 Open the Settings app and tap on the **Multi window** button under **Sound and display**

Multi window

2 Drag the **Multi window** button to **On**

← Multi window

Open in Multi window view
Open content in Multi window view automatically when an application is open in full screen view. Applications must support Multi window.

3 Press and hold on the **Back** button – see page 53 – (or on some phones, the **Recents** button) to access the Multi window selection bar down the right-hand side of the screen

4 Tap on an item to open it

Beware

Apps have to support Multi window mode to enable them to be used in this way.

63

Hot tip

Some newer phones have combined the Multi window functionality with the Recent Items page, and it is accessible through the **Recent Items** button.

...cont'd

5 Repeat the process in Steps 3 and 4 on page 63 to select another app and open it in Multi window view, e.g. two apps in one window

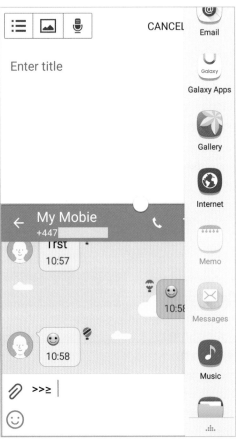

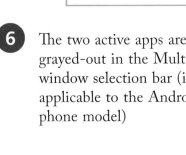

The currently active window in Multi window view is outlined by a thin blue line. Tap on the other window to make it the active one.

6 The two active apps are grayed-out in the Multi window selection bar (if applicable to the Android phone model)

Editing windows

It is possible to change the size of the windows in Multi window view. To do this:

1 When two apps are open in Multi window view, there is a dividing bar across the middle of the screen

On most Android phones with multi-windows, windows cannot be closed by dragging the button in Step 2 all the way to the bottom of the screen. To exit Multi window view, press the Home button and open another app, which should open on its own.

2 Press and hold on the white button on the dividing bar until it turns blue

3 Drag the button up or down accordingly to resize the windows

Locking Your Phone

Security is an important issue for any computing device and this applies to physical security as much as online security. For Android phones it is possible to place a digital lock on the screen so that only someone who knows the details of the lock can open it. There are different ways in which a lock can be set.

1 Tap on the **Settings** app

2 Tap on the **Lock screen** button, under **Sound and display**

Lock screen

3 The current method of **Screen lock** is displayed here. Tap on this to access the options

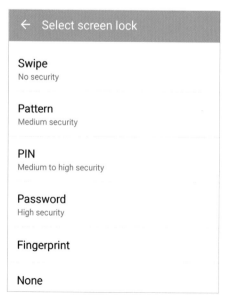

4 The methods for locking the screen are **Swipe**, **Pattern**, **PIN**, **Password**, **Fingerprint** (if applicable) and **None**. Tap on the required method to select it and set its attributes

Beware

The Swipe option is the least secure and is only really useful for avoiding items being activated accidentally when your phone is not in use; it is not a valid security method. The most secure method is a password containing letters, numbers and symbols.

5 For the **PIN** (or **Password**) option, enter your chosen PIN in the box and tap on the **Continue** button. Enter the PIN again for confirmation. This will then need to be entered whenever you want to unlock the phone

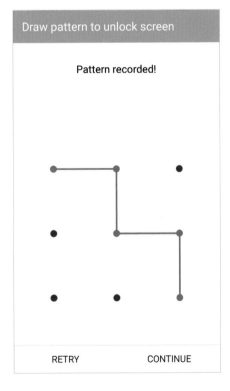

Enter PIN

PIN must contain at least 4 numbers.

•••|

CANCEL   CONTINUE

1	2 ABC	3 DEF
4 GHI	5 JKL	6 MNO
7 PQRS	8 TUV	9 WXYZ
⌫	0	Done

6 For the **Pattern** option, drag over the keypad to create the desired pattern, repeat to confirm, and then this will be enabled on your Lock screen

Draw pattern to unlock screen

Pattern recorded!

RETRY   CONTINUE

Hot tip

PIN stands for Personal Identification Number, and is a sequence of numbers chosen by and known only to you.

Hot tip

Whenever your phone goes to sleep it will need to be unlocked before you can use it again. Sleep mode can be activated by pressing the **On/Off** button once. After a period of inactivity it will go into Sleep mode automatically: the length of time until this happens can be specified within **Settings** > **Sound and display** > **Display** > **Sleep** (or **Screen timeout** on some phones).

Searching

Since Android is owned by Google, it is unsurprising that phones with this operating system come with the power of Google's search functionality. Items can be searched for within the phone itself, or you can perform searches on the web. This can be done by typing in the Google Search box and also by using the voice search option. To search for items on an Android phone:

1 The Google Search box is sometimes found on the Home  screen, or it can be accessed through the Google app, or added via a widget (see page 57)

2 Begin typing a word or phrase. As you type, corresponding suggestions will appear, both for on the web and for apps on the phone (if applicable)

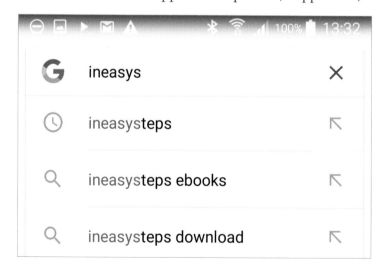

Don't forget

On some phones, the search option is indicated by a magnifying glass with the word Google next to it.

3 As you continue to type, the suggestions will become more defined

4 Tap on an app result to open it directly on your phone, or tap on this button on the keyboard to view the results from the web

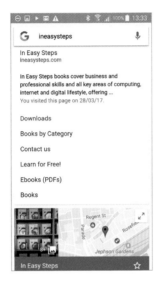

Voice search

To use the voice search functionality on your phone, instead of typing a search query:

The voice search functionality can also be used for items such as finding directions, setting alarms and finding photos on your phone.

1 Tap on the microphone button in the Search box

2 When the colored dots appear, speak the word or phrase for which you want to search

...cont'd

3 You can use voice search to find or open items on your phone or from the web. On your phone you can use voice search to open apps, such as your Gmail app

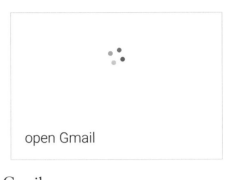

open Gmail

Don't forget

The phrase displayed in the voice search window is sometimes a summary of what you actually say. For instance, if you say, **"Please open Gmail app"**, the words **"open gmail"** may be displayed.

4 The app opens in the same way as if you had tapped on it from the Home screen

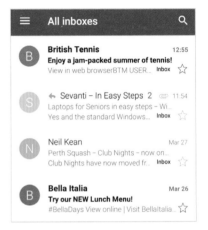

5 If you search for items on the web, Google will use your location (if enabled) and also your search history to give you more accurate results. For instance, if you search for "Italian restaurants" it will display the results for those closest to your location

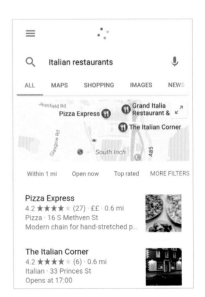

Google Assistant

One innovation from Google on some Android phones is the Google Assistant. This is a personal digital assistant that responds to voice commands. To use the Google Assistant:

1 Press and hold on the **Home** button to start setting up Google Assistant

2 Tap on the **Continue** button

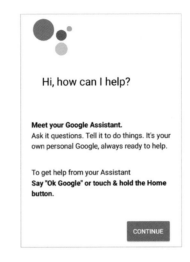

Once Google Assistant has been set up it is always available.

3 Tap on the **Done** button to allow the Assistant to offer suggestions based on what is on your screen and also what you have searched for previously

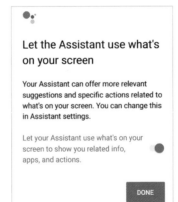

After you have set up Google Assistant, press and hold on the Home button to access it from any Home screen or app.

4 When the Assistant appears, you can ask it a query by speaking to it

...cont'd

5 Speak the query, such as "find the nearest coffee shop"

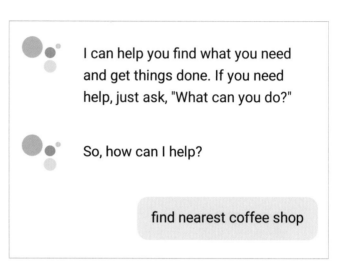

I can help you find what you need and get things done. If you need help, just ask, "What can you do?"

So, how can I help?

find nearest coffee shop

Hot tip

Google Assistant is an excellent option for finding locations when you are traveling. However, this requires a Wi-Fi or cellular network connection, with 3G or 4G.

Don't forget

Location must be checked on (**Settings** > **Network Connections** > **Location**) for these services to work.

6 The Assistant displays the results. There are also options for searching for the results over the web and viewing them on a map, if applicable

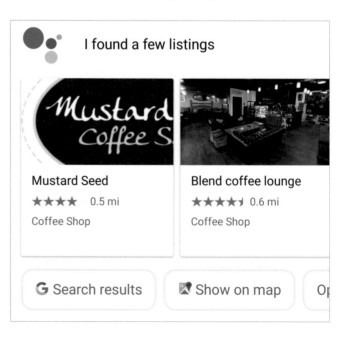

I found a few listings

Mustard Seed
★★★★ 0.5 mi
Coffee Shop

Blend coffee lounge
★★★★✦ 0.6 mi
Coffee Shop

G Search results   Show on map   Op

Ok Google

The Google Assistant also incorporates the "Ok Google" functionality, whereby you can use voice search commands from any screen. To set up Ok Google:

1 Once the Assistant has been set up, say "OK Google"

2 Tap on the **Get Started** button

GET STARTED

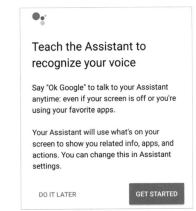

3 Say **OK Google** three times to train the Assistant. Once this is completed, Ok Google is set up

4 Say **OK Google** from any screen to access the Assistant and give it a command or a query

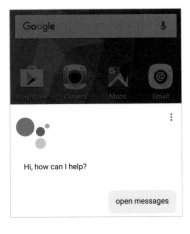

The Google Assistant can be used without training it to use your voice first. However, for Ok Google these steps have to be followed to set it up.

It may take Ok Google longer to recognize regional accents, but it should identify them after a bit of practice.

Don't forget

To use Google Feeds on your phone you have to be connected to the internet via Wi-Fi or cellular.

Don't forget

Google Feeds was previously known as Google Now, and some of this terminology remains in the app.

Hot tip

The Google Feeds page can be accessed from the Google app in Step 1 on the next page.

Using Google Feeds

We live in an age where we want the availability of as much up-to-date information as possible. On an Android phone, one option for this is Google Feeds. This is a digital assistant service that provides items such as the latest traffic information for your area, flight information or the results from your favorite sports team. The information displayed is tailored to your needs according to your location and the type of content that you access.

When Google Feeds is activated this also turns on your location history so that Google can make use of the location data that is collected by your phone, once you have authorized it to do so.

Google Feeds cards

The functionality of Google Feeds is provided by cards. These display up-to-date information for a variety of topics. You can apply your own specific settings for each card, and these will then display new information as it occurs. Cards appear when it is deemed that they are necessary, based on your location. So, if you are traveling in a different country, you will see a different range of cards from those when you are at home. Some of the most popular default cards include those for traveling to specific destinations (such as work) and sports cards.

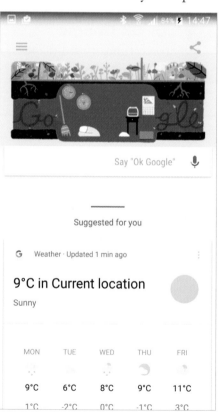

Accessing Google Feeds

By default, Google Feeds is not on (although it can be turned on during the initial setup process for your phone). To activate it so that it works for you in the background:

1 Tap on the **Google** app

2 Tap on the **Get Started** button at the bottom of the screen

> Want answers before you ask?
> See weather, traffic and other info when you need it on Google
>
> **GET STARTED**

3 Tap on the **Set Up** button at the bottom of the screen

SET UP

Google Feeds also accesses your web history, in order to provide you with as much relevant information as possible. This is stored as part of your Google Account and can be accessed by logging in with your account details at the website, **accounts.google.com** and accessing the **My Activity** section.

4 Tap on the **Yes, I'm In** button on the **Set up the feed?** page

YES, I'M IN

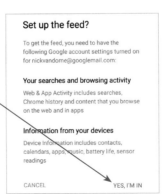

> Set up the feed?
>
> To get the feed, you need to have the following Google account settings turned on for nickvandome@googlemail.com:
>
> **Your searches and browsing activity**
> Web & App Activity includes searches, Chrome history and content that you browse on the web and in apps
>
> **Information from your devices**
> Device Information includes contacts, calendars, apps, music, battery life, sensor readings
>
> CANCEL   YES, I'M IN

Some of the Google Feeds cards include: weather, traffic, sports, public transport, next appointment, news updates, stocks, and travel. There is also a range of Gmail cards that can be used to track items that have been bought online, and use Gmail for the confirmation email, such as packages, restaurant bookings and flights.

...cont'd

Around Google Feeds

When you first activate Google Feeds you will see the Home screen. This is where your cards will show up, and from where you can access all of the settings for individual cards, such as selecting the way in which weather updates are displayed.

Don't forget

The Google Search box is located at the top of the Google Feeds Home screen. This can be used to search your Google Feeds cards, your phone and also the web.

1 Active cards are shown on the Home screen

Hot tip

To delete a card, swipe it left or right off the screen. The card will come back the next time that the item is updated. To remove a card completely, click the **Never show...** option in Step 3.

2 Tap here to view the card's individual settings

3 Specific settings can be applied for individual cards, such as the way in which the Weather card displays its information

Customizing Google Feeds

Google Feeds can be customized so that you get exactly the type of information that you want. To do this:

1 Tap on the **Menu** button at the top of the Google Feeds window

2 Tap on the **Customize** button

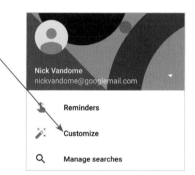

3 Tap on the items at the top of the window to specify the way in which directions are displayed

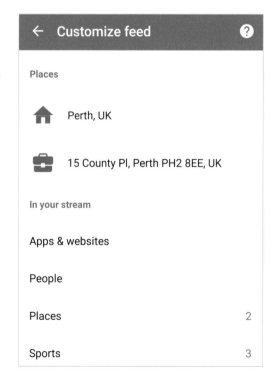

The **Settings** option (further down the panel in Step 2) provides a range of settings that can be applied for Google Search and also Google Feeds.

...cont'd

4 For the items in Step 3, tap on a category and tap on an option to add another card, such as **Add a team**

5 Enter the name of the required item. For some options, suggestions will appear as you type

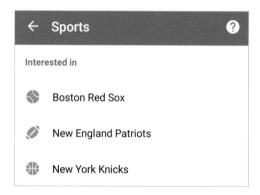

Add a team

new york k|

New York K**nicks**

Beware

Only teams can be added from the Sports section on Google Feeds, not individual sportspeople.

6 The selected item is included as something in which you are interested

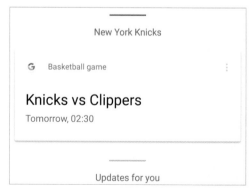

← Sports

Interested in

Boston Red Sox

New England Patriots

New York Knicks

7 A card for the selected item is added to the Google Feeds Home screen. This can include items such as scores,

New York Knicks

G Basketball game

Knicks vs Clippers
Tomorrow, 02:30

Updates for you

reports and related videos, and also shows the card's Settings button

5 Calls and Contacts

This chapter concentrates on using an Android phone to make and receive calls, and also how to add the contact details of people who have phoned or texted you.

80 Adding Contacts

82 Saving Contacts from Calls

83 Saving Contacts from Texts

84 From Phone to SIM

86 Editing Contacts

88 Making a Call

90 Receiving a Call

93 Setting Ringtones

Adding Contacts

Given the range of uses to which you can put your Android phone, it is sometimes overlooked that one of its original functions is to make phone calls to people. This can be done by typing a number directly into the phone dialer (see page 88). However, it is generally better to first add contacts to your phone and then you can use these details to keep in touch with them in a variety of ways. To add a contact:

The Contacts option in Step 2 can also be accessed from the **Phone** app.

1 Tap on the **Contacts** app

2 By default, the Contacts app will only show the details of the SIM card currently installed. Tap on the **+** button to add a new contact to your Contacts list

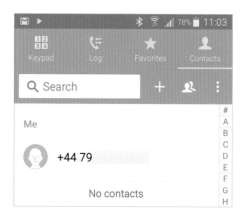

80

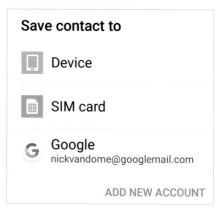

If you have a Google Account, contacts can be added here too so that they are available from the Contacts app and the Phone app.

3 Select where you want to store the contact. Generally, it is better to store Contacts on the **SIM card**, rather than **Device**, so if you get a new phone you can move all of your contacts by simply transferring the SIM card

4 Enter the details for the new contact and tap on the **Save** button. (Saving to the SIM allows for less information about a contact to be stored than when the **Device** option is selected)

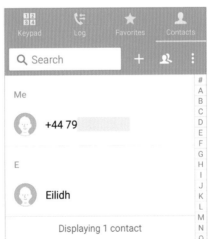

Hot tip

If you save a contact to the SIM card, it will be available if you put the SIM card into another phone.

5 The new contact is added to the Contacts app (which is also accessed from the **Contacts** tab in the **Phone** app)

6 Tap on a contact to see their details. Tap on the envelope icon to create a text message for the selected contact, the phone icon to make a call to them, or the video icon to make a video call

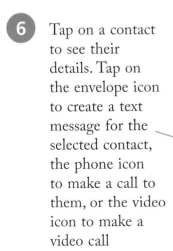

Don't forget

When you receive a call, accept it by pressing the green phone button and dragging it to the right. To reject a call, drag the red button to the left.

Don't forget

The **Log** page shows all of the calls and texts that you have received.

Hot tip

To add a contact from a record in the Log, you can also just click on it and select **Add to Contacts** or **Create Contact**.

Saving Contacts from Calls

Another quick way to add a contact is to ask someone to phone you so that you can then copy their number directly from your phone to your Contacts. You do not even have to answer the phone to do this.

1 Once someone has phoned, tap on the **Phone** button

2 Tap on the **Log** button. The call or text will be displayed. Tap on the **Menu** button

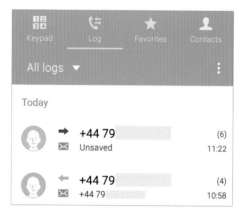

3 Tap on the **Select** button to select one of the items in the Log section

Select

4 Tap on one of the records to select it

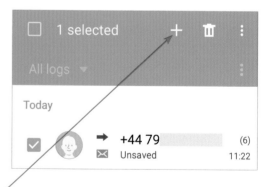

5 Tap on the **+** button and save the contact in the same way as in Steps 4 and 5 on the following page

Saving Contacts from Texts

Contacts can also be saved from text messages:

1 When you have been sent a text, open the Messages app to view it

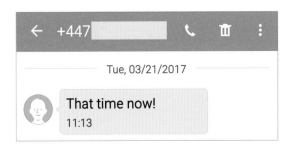

2 Tap on the **Menu** button

3 Tap on the **Add to contacts** button

Add to contacts

4 Tap on the **Create Contact** button

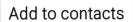

5 The number will already be inserted, so add the name and tap on the **Save** button to save the contact

Hot tip

Someone can send you a blank text, just to add their details to your contacts.

Hot tip

If someone is already in your contacts, but you do not have their cell/mobile number included, or you want to update an existing number, tap on the **Update Existing** button in Step 4 to add the number to their existing details.

From Phone to SIM

Sometimes you may end up with contacts on your phone (if you have selected to save them onto your **Device** rather than **SIM**) and you will want to transfer them to your SIM card. This is useful if you are going to transfer your SIM card to another phone. To do this:

Hot tip

If a contact is added without a mobile phone number, the icon in Step 2 will be colored blue.

1 Tap on the **Contacts** app

2 Tap on the **Contacts** tab. Contacts that have a gold icon next to them have been saved onto the SIM card; ones with a green icon 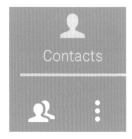 have been saved onto the device (colors can vary on different Android devices)

3 Tap on the **Menu** button at the top of the window

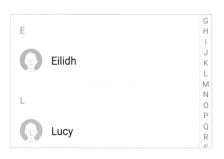

4 Tap on the **Settings** button Settings

5 Tap on the **Contacts** button

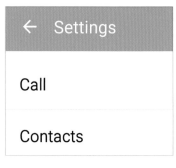

6 Tap on the **Import/ Export contacts** button

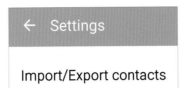

Settings

Import/Export contacts

Hot tip

7 Tap on the **Export to SIM card** button to start the transfer (other import and export options can also be used)

Import/Export contacts

Import from device storage

Export to device storage

Import from SIM card

Export to SIM card

Contact information can also be copied from the SIM card to the phone. This is done by tapping on the **Import from SIM card** button in Step 7. This is a useful option if you want to copy numbers from a SIM card that you have used on another device, and so have them saved on your Android phone as well as the SIM card.

8 Tap on a contact to select it and tap on the **Done** button at the top of the window

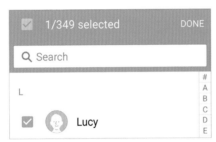

1/349 selected   DONE

Q Search

L

☑ Lucy

9 Since more information can be stored for a device contact than for a SIM one, some details you may have entered may be lost

Copy to SIM

Some information might be lost. Continue?

CANCEL   OK

when moving the contact to the SIM. A dialog box appears asking if you want to continue. If you do, tap on the **OK** button

Don't forget

To copy all of the eligible contacts to the SIM, tap on this button at the top of the window.

10 The contact is added to the SIM card on your phone, and your Contacts list displays this too (indicated by the gold icon)

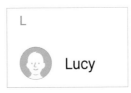

L

Lucy

☑ 261/348 selected

Q Search

Editing Contacts

Once contacts have been added to your Android phone you can still edit their details, whether they have been added to the phone or the SIM card, although a wider range of information can be added to a contact on the phone.

1 Tap on the **Contacts** app

2 Access a contact and tap on their name to view their details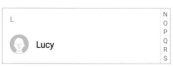

3 The current details are displayed. Tap on the **Edit** button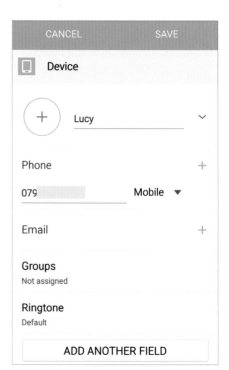

If you have downloaded messaging apps, such as WhatsApp, the information from your Contacts list will be synced with this and any of your contacts who are using the service will automatically be displayed in the messaging app, if you agree to this when you install the WhatsApp app.

86

4 Edit the details as required. Contacts that have been added to the phone (**Device**) have a greater range of fields for information. If the contact has only been added to the SIM card, the only fields available will be for Name and Phone number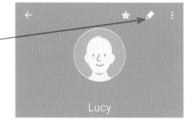

5 Tap on the **Ringtone** button to select a specific ringtone

Ringtone
Default

6 Tap on the **Add Another Field** button to select other fields to include

ADD ANOTHER FIELD

7 Tap on the required additional fields and tap on the **OK** button

Add another field

Phonetic name ☐

Organization ☑

IM ☐

Address ☑

Notes ☐

Nickname ☐

Website ☑

Internet call ☐

CANCEL   OK

87

8 The additional fields are added and can have content added to them. Tap on the **Save** button to save the editing changes

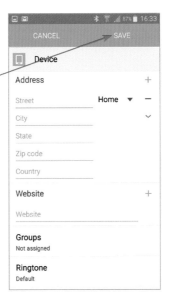

Making a Call

Once you have added contacts to your phone there are a number of ways in which you can phone them.

Typing a name

You can make a call by accessing the phone dialer and typing a contact's number on the keypad. To do this:

1 Tap on the **Phone** app

2 Tap on the **Keypad** tab at the top of the screen. Type the person's number on the keypad. As the number is entered, corresponding names will be displayed from your Contacts list

3 Tap on the contact's name to display their full number

4 Tap on the **Call** button to call the number

...cont'd

Searching for a contact

Once you have added contacts to your Contacts list you can access them and then call them. To do this:

1   Tap on the **Phone** app

2   Tap on the **Contacts** tab. At the top of the Contacts list is a Search box

3   Tap on the Search box and type a name you want to find

4   All matching results are shown. The more characters of a

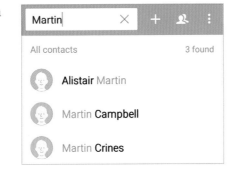

name that you type, the more the search results will be narrowed down. Tap on the contact you want to call

Making a quick call

It is also possible to place a call to a contact in your Contacts list, just using one swipe. To do this:

1   Access the Contacts list

2   Swipe to the right on the contact's name. The green **Call** button appears and the call is connected automatically

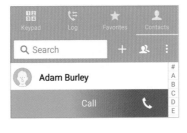

Hot tip

Swipe to the left on a contact's name to send them a text message, rather than make a call.

Receiving a Call

When you receive a call, the caller's name will show up on the screen, accompanied by a ringtone (see pages 93-94).

Hot tip

On some Android models, if the caller has sent you any text messages, the latest one will be displayed on the Incoming call screen.

Hot tip

Tap on the **Reject call with message** button in Step 2 to reject the call but send the caller a text message instead.

✉ Reject call with message

1 When a call is received, the caller's name is displayed (if they have been added as a contact) along with their phone number. If their photo has been added to their contact details, this will be displayed too

2 Swipe the green button to the right to accept a call, or swipe the red button to the left to reject it

3 If you are using another app when a call is received, the full-size window is minimized to a smaller one. Tap on **Answer**, **Answer on speaker**, or **Reject**

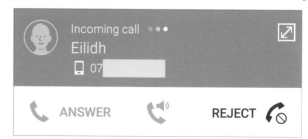

4 Once a call has been accepted, these buttons appear at the bottom of the window, when in full screen

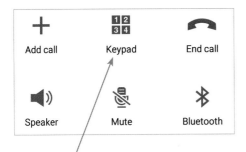

✚	🔢	📞
Add call	Keypad	End call
🔊	🔇	✳
Speaker	Mute	Bluetooth

5 Tap on the **Keypad** button to access a keypad that can be used during the call, i.e. if you are selecting options during an automated call

1	2 ABC	3 DEF
4 GHI	5 JKL	6 MNO
7 PQRS	8 TUV	9 WXYZ
✳	0	#
✚ Add call	🔢 Hide	📞 End call
🔊 Speaker	🔇 Mute	✳ Bluetooth

Hot tip

Tap on the **Bluetooth** button in Step 4 to connect your phone to a Bluetooth headset or headphones, so that you can take the call hands-free.

6 Tap on the **Speaker** button to activate the speaker so that you can hear the call without holding the phone to your ear

🔊 **Speaker**

7 The Home screen, or other apps, can be accessed during a call by pressing the Home button, in which case the call window is minimized at the top of the screen

...cont'd

8 During a call in full screen, tap on the **Menu** button at the top of the call window

9 Select options for the call, including putting it on **Hold**, viewing the caller in **Contacts**, sending them a **Memo** or a **Message** and **Personalize** the call sound for the specific caller

Hold
Contacts
Memo
Messages
Personalize call sound
SIM services
Settings

10 Tap on the **End call** button to end the current call

End call

11 Once a call has been ended, tap on these buttons to **View contact** or call them back with a **Video call**, **Call** or **Message**

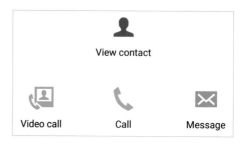

Setting Ringtones

Ringtones were one of the original must-have accessories that helped transform the way people looked at mobile/cell phones. Android phones have a range of ringtones that can be used, and you can also download and install thousands more. To use the default ringtones:

① Tap on the **Settings** app

Settings

② Tap on the **Sounds and notifications** button under **Sound and display**

Sounds and notifications

③ Tap on the **Ringtones** button for ringtones for when you receive a phone call (tap on **Notification ringtone** for other items, such as text messages)

Ringtones
Over the Horizon

④ Tap on one of the options to hear a preview

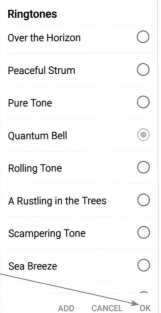

Ringtones

Over the Horizon ○

Peaceful Strum ○

Pure Tone ○

Quantum Bell ◉

Rolling Tone ○

A Rustling in the Trees ○

Scampering Tone ○

Sea Breeze ○

ADD   CANCEL   OK

⑤ With the desired tone selected, tap on the **OK** button to select the ringtone for your phone

Hot tip

You can use your own music as a ringtone, providing the music is in an appropriate format and not locked because of digital rights issues. Tap on the **Add** button in Step 5 and select the required music from the Play Music app, or any ringtone that you have downloaded, then tap **Done** to select.

...cont'd

Getting more ringtones

While the default ringtones will serve a perfectly good purpose, there is also a wealth of sounds and music that can be downloaded and used as ringtones. This can be done through the Google Play Store:

Beware

Experimenting with different ringtones can be good fun, but after a while you may find that they can become slightly irritating for you, and those nearby.

Don't forget

If the new ringtone does not appear automatically in the list in Step 5 on the previous page, tap on the **Add** button to select it and add it to the system list of ringtones.

1 Access the Google Play Store app. Tap on the Search box and enter "ringtones" to see the available options

2 Tap on one of the search results

3 Tap on one of the ringtone apps to download it

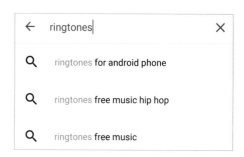

4 Open the app and download one of the ringtones in the app. This will then be available in the list in Step 4 on page 93. Select it and tap on the **OK** button to use it as a ringtone

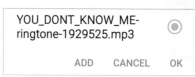

6 Using the Keyboard

This chapter looks at entering text and data with the keyboard on an Android phone, focusing on the widely available Google keyboard: Gboard.

96 Keyboards with Android

97 Selecting Keyboards

98 About the Google Keyboard

100 Keyboard Settings

102 Gboard Shortcuts Bar

104 General Keyboard Shortcuts

105 Adding Text

106 Working with Text

Keyboards with Android

All Android phones have a keyboard, for inputting text and data, and the vast majority of them are virtual ones, i.e. they appear on the screen, rather than an actual physical keyboard. Different phone manufacturers add their own keyboards to their specific handsets, and this is usually the default keyboard that appears. However, different keyboards can be downloaded from the Play Store, including the Google keyboard (Gboard) which is a good, multi-purpose Android keyboard. To download different keyboards:

As the Google keyboard is produced by Google, it can be considered the default Android keyboard and is used for the examples in this chapter.

1 Access the Play Store and type "android keyboard" into the Search box

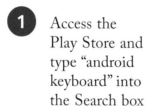
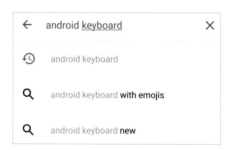

2 Tap on one of the search results to view the keyboard app and download and install it, if required

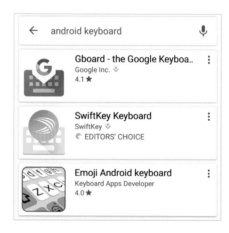

3 The keyboard app will be added to the next available Home screen. Tap on it to set it up and also access its settings once setup is completed

Selecting Keyboards

Several different keyboards can be installed and used on your Android phone. Keyboards can be changed at any time and different ones selected. To do this:

1 Tap on the **Settings** app

2 Tap on the **Language and input** button under **System**

3 The keyboard currently being used is listed under **Keyboards and input methods > Default**. Tap on the **Default** button to select a different keyboard

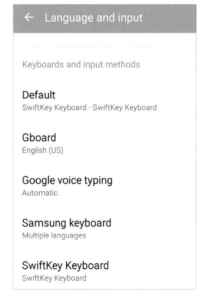

4 Tap on another keyboard to select it and make it the default one currently being used

Tap on the items below the Default button to access settings for each item, i.e. the different available keyboards.

Tap on the **Set Up Input Methods** button in Step 4 to enable or disable keyboards. The keyboards will be listed: check **On** or **Off** the checkbox next to a keyboard to enable or disable it.

About the Google Keyboard

As with other Android keyboards, the Google keyboard (Gboard) can be used for a variety of actions:

- Entering text with a messaging app, word processing app, email app or a notes app.

- Entering a web address.

- Entering information into a form.

- Entering a password.

Viewing the keyboard

When you attempt one of the tasks above, the keyboard appears before you can enter any text or numbers:

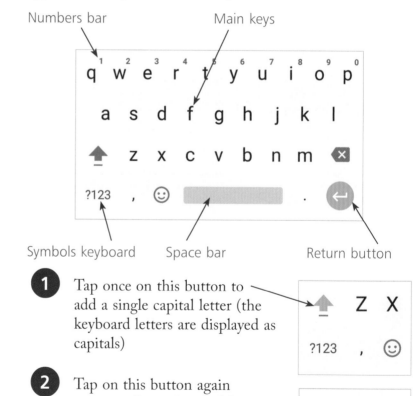

Numbers bar   Main keys

Symbols keyboard   Space bar   Return button

Don't forget

When using the keyboard for normal text or data entry, it only requires a light touch: you do not have to press very hard on the keys.

Don't forget

The Numbers bar on the Gboard is permanently available as part of the top row of letters: press and hold on a letter to add the number above it.

Don't forget

Caps Lock means that all the letters will be entered as capital letters.

1 Tap once on this button to add a single capital letter (the keyboard letters are displayed as capitals)

2 Tap on this button again to create **Caps Lock** (if caps are activated as in Step 1, double-tap if not). This is indicated by the solid green line below the arrow

3 Tap once on this button to back delete an item

4 Tap once on this button to access the **Symbols** keyboard option

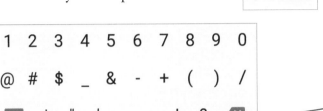

Tap on this button to access the number pad for entering numerical data.

5 Tap on this button to access the second page of the **Symbols** keyboard

Sometimes the button in Step 5 is **1/2** or **2/2**. Tap these buttons to move between the Symbols pages.

6 Tap once on this button on either of the symbols keyboards above to return to the standard **QWERTY** option

7 Tap once on the **Back** button to hide the keyboard. If the keyboard is hidden, tap once on one of the input options, e.g. in a text box for entering text in a form, to show it again

If you are entering a password, or details into a form, the keyboard will have a **Go** or **Send** button that can be used to activate the information that has been entered.

Keyboard Settings

There are a number of options for setting up the functionality of the Google keyboard. These can be accessed in two ways:

Don't forget

Tap on the **Preferences** button in Step 3 to access a range of options for the keys on the keyboard, and the layout and key press options such as for sounds and vibrations for when keys are pressed.

Don't forget

Some keyboards have a setting for **Predictive text**. This is a function where words are suggested as you type them: as more letters are added to the word, the suggestion becomes more defined. In the Gboard app, this functionality is provided by the **Show suggestions** option (see next page).

1 Tap on the **Gboard** app, or

2 Press and hold on the comma button on the keyboard and tap on the **Gboard keyboard settings** option

?123   ,

3 The full list of keyboard settings is displayed

4 Tap on the **Languages** option to select different languages

5 Tap on the **Theme** option to select a colored theme for the keyboard

6 Tap on the **Dictionary** option for creating a personal dictionary, which lets you add your own words to the dictionary, and also shortcuts for frequently used words or names

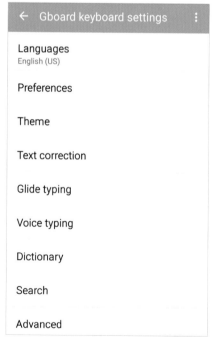

Gboard

Gboard

Languages

Gboard keyboard settings

← Gboard keyboard settings

Languages
English (US)

Preferences

Theme

Text correction

Glide typing

Voice typing

Dictionary

Search

Advanced

7 Tap on the **Text correction** button shown on the previous page, to access options for working with text as it is being written

8 Drag **On** or **Off** the buttons for **Show suggestions**, **Next-word suggestions**, **Block offensive words**, **Show emoji suggestions** and **Suggest contact names**

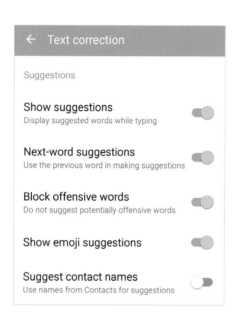

← Text correction

Suggestions

Show suggestions
Display suggested words while typing

Next-word suggestions
Use the previous word in making suggestions

Block offensive words
Do not suggest potentially offensive words

Show emoji suggestions

Suggest contact names
Use names from Contacts for suggestions

The **Show suggestions** option displays suggested words as you type (tap on one to select it); **Next-word suggestions** displays a possible next word, based on the one just used; **Show emoji suggestions** displays a suggested emoji to replace a word; and **Suggest contact names** displays names from the Contacts app.

101

9 Scroll down the **Text correction** page to access options for **Auto-correction**, **Auto capitalization** and **Double-space period**. Drag the buttons **On** or **Off** as required

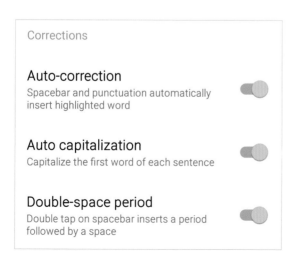

Corrections

Auto-correction
Spacebar and punctuation automatically insert highlighted word

Auto capitalization
Capitalize the first word of each sentence

Double-space period
Double tap on spacebar inserts a period followed by a space

The **Auto-correction** option lets you insert the currently highlighted word by tapping on the spacebar; **Auto capitalization** automatically inserts a capital letter at the start of a new sentence; **Double-space period** adds a period/full stop when the spacebar is tapped twice.

Gboard Shortcuts Bar

At the top of the Gboard keyboard (and most other Android keyboards) is a shortcuts bar, if suggestions are turned on (see page 101). This includes the Google Search button and also additional functionality for the keyboard.

Google Search button

The Search button on the Gboard can be used for general search queries and also for finding information about the text message or email which you are writing:

Hot tip

When a search result is shared using the **Share** button in Step 3, it is added to the current message, including a link to the web page from where the information was obtained.

1 Write a text message or email and tap on the **Google** Search button at the left-hand side of the Gboard shortcuts bar

2 Enter a search request and tap on the Search button on the keyboard

3 The search result is displayed. The information can be added manually to a message and also included in the message, using the **Share** button

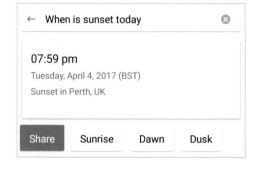

...cont'd

More shortcuts bar functionality

The Gboard shortcuts bar also has a range of other functionality that can be accessed from the Google button at the top of the keyboard:

1 Tap on this button to access **Google Translate**. A text box appears, and text can be entered into it for translation

2 Tap on this button to select a **Theme** for the keyboard, e.g. text and background color

3 Tap on this button to minimize the keyboard to make it easier to use one-handed

Don't forget

Voice typing can also be accessed from the shortcuts bar by tapping on this button.

4 Tap on this arrow to swap the minimized keyboard from right to left

5 Tap on this button to access the **Gboard Settings**

6 Tap on this button to exit the shortcuts bar

General Keyboard Shortcuts

Because of the size of the keyboard on an Android phone, some keys have duplicate functionality, in order to fit in all of the options. This includes dual function keys, spacebar shortcuts and accented letters.

Much of this functionality is accessed by pressing and holding on the keys, rather than just tapping on them once.

Dual functions

If a key has more than one character, both items can be accessed from the same button.

1 Press and hold on the period/full stop key to view the additional options. Slide your finger over the character, to insert it

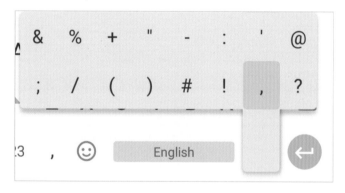

Hot tip

Press and hold on compatible letters on the keyboard to access accented versions for different languages. These include the a, c, e, i, o, s and u keys.

Spacebar shortcut

The spacebar can also be used for a useful shortcut: at the end of a sentence, double-tap on the spacebar to add a full stop/period and a space, ready for the start of the next sentence, if this is enabled as shown in Step 9 on page 101.

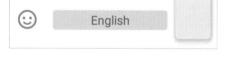

The end.

Adding Text

Once you have applied the keyboard settings that you require, you can start entering text, in appropriate apps:

1 Tap once in a text box to activate the keyboard. Start typing with the keyboard. The text will appear at the point where you tapped on the screen

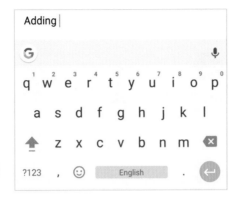

2 If **Show suggestions** is enabled, suggestions appear above the keyboard as you type a word. Tap once on a word on the suggestions bar to include it

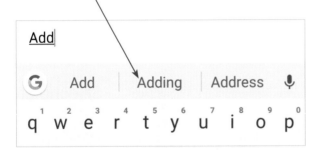

3 If **Next-word suggestions** is enabled, suggestions appear after the last word entered

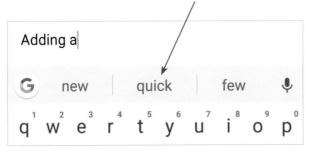

Use the back delete button to remove unwanted text once it has been added.

If **Show suggestions** is enabled in the keyboard settings (see page 101), **Next-word suggestions** is automatically enabled.

See Chapter Seven for details about adding text in a text message.

Working with Text

Once text has been entered it can be selected, copied, cut and pasted, either within an app or between apps.

Selecting text

To select text and perform tasks on it:

1 Tap anywhere to set the insertion point for adding or editing text

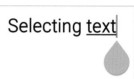

2 Drag the marker to move the insertion point

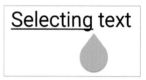

3 Double-tap or press and hold on a word to select it and activate the selection handles

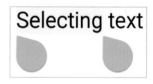

4 Drag the handles to change the text that is selected

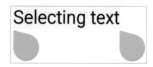

5 Tap on these buttons to **Cut** or **Copy** the selected text

6 Locate the point at which you want to insert the text, and press and hold. Tap on **Paste** to add the text

Don't forget

To select all of the text in a text box, press and hold on the text, then tap on the Select all button in Step 6.

7 Messaging and Email

Text messaging is an important way for contacting family and friends. This chapter shows how to use texts and enhance them with emojis and attachments.

108 Texting Contacts

110 Using a 3x4 Keyboard

112 Using Emojis

114 Adding Attachments

115 Glide Typing

116 Changing the Skin

118 Setting Up Email

120 Using Gmail

122 Going Hands-Free

Hot tip

When you send a text message to someone this starts a conversation thread. To delete a thread, in the **Messages** app, press and hold on the conversation thread, and tap on the Trash icon that appears.

Don't forget

Apps such as WhatsApp and Messenger (Facebook) can be used for texting people. This is known as "internet messaging", and one of its useful features is being able to create text groups, so that everyone in a group can see what the other members are saying. It is usually free to message people with these apps.

Texting Contacts

As with phone calls, it is possible to use your contacts to send text messages in a number of ways:

Finding a contact in Messages

To text a contact directly from the Messages app:

1 Tap on the **Messages** app

2 Tap on the **New message** button

3 Tap on this button next to the **Enter recipients** box to access your contacts

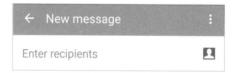

4 Tap on the required name to select it and tap on the **Done** button

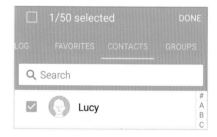

5 Compose the text and tap on the **Send** button

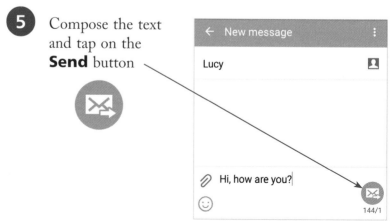

Texting from your Contacts list

You can also text a contact directly from your Contacts list:

1 Tap on the **Contacts** app

2 Find the contact you want to text

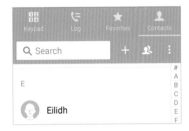

Don't forget

To call a contact instead of sending them a text, tap on the phone number (underneath the Message icon), or the Video call button if you want to make a video call.

3 Tap on the contact's name and tap on the **Message** button. A new text message is opened with the contact's name already inserted

Quick contact messaging

As with a phone call, it is possible to quickly start a text message with a contact with one swipe. To do this:

1 Tap on the **Contacts** app

2 Find the contact you want to text

3 Swipe to the left on the contact's name. The orange **Message** button 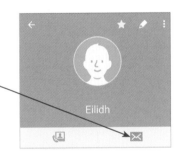 appears and opens up a new text message with the contact's name already inserted as the recipient

Beware

When you are accessing a contact's details by tapping on their name, be careful not to swipe the button instead, as it could activate the quick messaging or calling function by mistake.

Beware

The 3x4 keyboard is only available in portrait mode: if you change to landscape mode, the QWERTY keyboard appears instead.

Using a 3x4 Keyboard

Some keyboards have a 3x4 keyboard option (but not the Gboard keyboard). This is smaller than the QWERTY keyboard, and has three or four letters assigned to each button. To access the 3x4 keyboard:

1 Select **Settings** > **System** > **Language and input** and tap on

←   Language and input

Samsung keyboard
Multiple languages

the keyboard with which you want to apply the 3x4 setting

2 If more than one keyboard language is being used, tap on the one to apply the 3x4 settings to (tap on the

Input languages

English(UK)
3x4 keyboard

English(US)
Qwerty keyboard

+   Select input languages

Select input languages button to add more keyboard languages)

3 Tap on the **3x4 keyboard** option

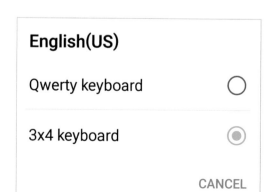

English(US)

Qwerty keyboard   ○

3x4 keyboard   ◉

CANCEL

Using a 3x4 keyboard
To enter content with a 3x4 keyboard:

1 Tap on each button successive times to insert each letter, e.g. tap four times on the **pqrs** button to

insert an **s**. If you then want to insert another letter from the same button, wait a couple of seconds or else it may overwrite the one you inserted originally

2 Tap on this button to access the number and special character options (numbers can also be inserted by pressing and holding on the associated key for a couple of seconds)

3 Tap on this button to add a new line

4 Tap on this button to add capitals (tap once for a single capital letter, and double-tap for Caps Lock)

5 Tap on this button to back delete an item

6 Tap on this button to access the keyboard's settings

Hot tip

Press and hold on one of the 3x4 keyboard buttons to enter the number in the top right-hand corner of the button, rather than entering a letter.

111

Using Emojis

Emojis (small graphical symbols) are becoming increasingly common in text messages and on social media. Some people love them, while others loathe them, but they are now a regular feature in digital communications. Whatever your views on them, there are a number of ways to insert them:

Quick insert

Emojis can be inserted directly from the Messages text box:

1 Compose a text message, and at any point, tap on the emoji symbol next to the message

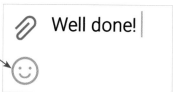

2 Tap on an item on the top bar to view the emojis in the panel below. Swipe up and down or left and right to view all of the emojis in a category. Tap on an emoji to add it

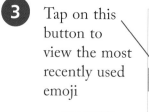

3 Tap on this button to view the most recently used emoji

Smileys

Emojis were originally created from keyboard symbols. These were known as "smileys", and they can still be used from the emoji keyboard:

Don't forget

Smileys are a good way to see the symbols that make up each item.

1 Compose a text message and tap on this button on the bottom toolbar

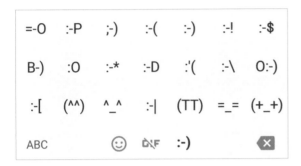

2 Tap on a smiley to add it to the current message

Searching for emojis

There are hundreds of emojis, and it can sometimes be difficult to find the right one. However, it is possible to search for emojis using keywords:

Hot tip

Smileys are a good option for recipients who do not have a phone that can display graphical emojis. However, some phones will render a smiley as a graphical symbol.

1 Tap in the **Search emoji** box and enter a keyword

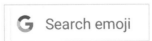

2 The matching emojis are displayed. Tap on one to add it to the current message

Adding Attachments

Text messages do not have to only include words; it is also possible to attach a variety of other items, such as photos, music tracks and videos:

1 Open a new text message and tap on the **Attach** button

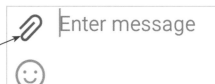

114

2 Select the type of content you want to add to your text, e.g. photos, videos, music or recorded audio

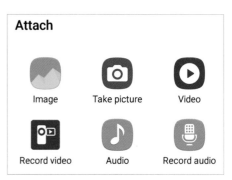

3 Select the app from where you want to select the content to attach to the message

4 Select the required item, which will be added to the message (text can also then be added)

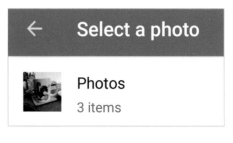

Glide Typing

Another way of creating texts with the Google keyboard is with the Glide typing option. This is where you swipe over the keyboard to create words, rather than tapping on the individual letters. To do this:

1 Select **Settings > System > Language and input > Gboard** and tap on the **Glide typing** option

2 Drag the **Enable glide typing** and **Show gesture trail** buttons to **On**

Beware

Glide typing is best used for short messages, rather than trying to write anything of length.

3 When you create a message, drag over the keyboard with a finger to add the letters for the words you want to create. If the **Show gesture trail** option in Step 2 is **On**, a colored line is visible as your finger moves over the letters. If you need to create a double letter, make a circular motion on the relevant letter on the keyboard

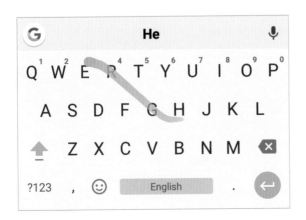

Changing the Skin

The color scheme (or "skin") used for text message conversations is another area that you can customize:

1 Open the **Settings** app, tap on **Applications**, then select **Messages**

Messages

2 Tap on the **Display** option

Hot tip

Use styles and backgrounds that provide a good contrast between text and the background color.

3 Tap on the **Bubble style** or the **Background style** options

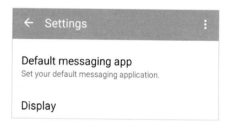

4 For the **Bubble style**, the current style is displayed, with additional options in the panel at the bottom of the screen

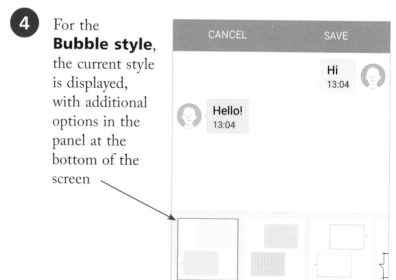

5 Swipe along the bottom panel to view the options, and tap on one to select it

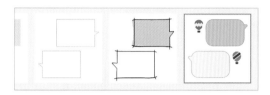

6 The selection is displayed at the top of the screen. Tap on the **Save** button to apply it

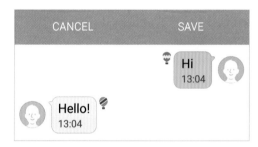

Bubble and Background styles can be changed as often as you like, for variety in your text messages.

7 Select the **Background style** in the same way as for the Bubble style, and tap on the **Save** button

Bubble and Background styles only appear on your own phone; recipients will apply their own styles.

Setting Up Email

Email is still one of the main forms of electronic communication. Most Android phone manufacturers include their own Email app for adding email accounts, but the Gmail app can also be used for this, in addition to being used for emails from a Google Account. To add an email account:

Don't forget

Email accounts can also be set up from the Settings app, under **Accounts > Add account**.

Hot tip

Usually, email providers have their own apps, e.g. Outlook.com for Microsoft accounts, Yahoo! Mail etc.

118

1 Tap on the **Gmail** app

Gmail

2 Tap on the Gmail **Menu** button in the top left-hand corner

≡ Inbox

3 Swipe down the menu and tap on the **Settings** button

⚙ Settings

4 Tap on the **Add account** option to add a new account that can be used with the Gmail app

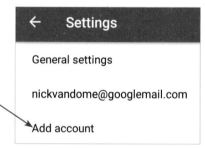

← Settings

General settings

nickvandome@googlemail.com

Add account

5 Tap on the type of account that you want to add. Tap on the **Other** option if your email account provider is not on the list

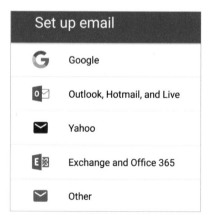

Set up email

G Google

O Outlook, Hotmail, and Live

Yahoo

E Exchange and Office 365

Other

6 Enter the email address of the account you want to add, and then tap on the **Next** button

Add your email address

Enter your email
nickvandome@mac.com

MANUAL SETUP

<   NEXT >

Don't forget

Numerous email accounts can be added to the Gmail app.

7 Enter the password for the account you want to add, and then tap on the **Next** button

nickvandome@mac.com

Password
........| 👁̸

<   NEXT >

Don't forget

8 Select the options for the account, including those for notifications when emails arrive, syncing the account and downloading attachments. Tap on the **Next** button to finish setting up the new account

Account options

Sync frequency:

Every 15 minutes   ▾

☑ Notify me when email arrives

☑ Sync email from this account

☑ Automatically download attachments when connected to Wi-Fi

<   NEXT >

When an email account is synced, any items that are saved online are copied to the phone, so that the two locations display the same information.

Using Gmail

Accessing emails

Emails from different email accounts can all be viewed and managed using Gmail. To do this:

1 Tap on the **Gmail** app

2 By default, Gmail should open at your Inbox, with your emails displayed. Tap on one to open it

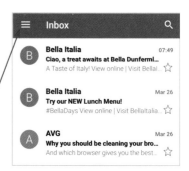

Hot tip

The Menu in Step 3 has options for accessing different mailboxes (Sent, Outbox and Drafts) and also options for adding labels to specific emails so that they can be searched for using these labels.

3 Tap on the **Menu** button then tap on the **All inboxes** button to see emails for all of the accounts that have been added to Gmail

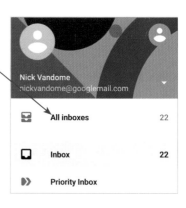

4 All of your emails are displayed within the same Inbox

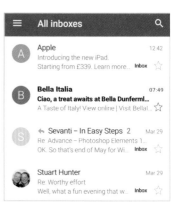

Hot tip

Swipe down from the top of the screen to manually refresh the emails in your Inbox.

Creating email

Once you have set up an email account you can use it to
send and receive all of your emails on your Android phone.
To send an email:

1 Tap on the **Gmail** app

2 Tap on the **Compose** button

3 Compose the
email by adding a
recipient, subject
and body text

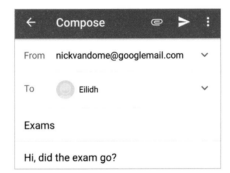

If a recipient is in your
Contacts app, their
full email address will
appear as you type
their name in Step 3,
providing the email
address is included
in their entry in the
Contacts app.

121

4 To format text,
press on a word
to select it. Tap
on the **Format**
button to access
the formatting toolbar

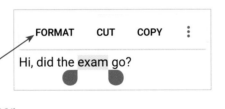

Tap on the **Attach**
button on the top
bar to include photos,
video or music files in
your email.

5 Select the
required
formatting for
the selected
word, including
bold, italics, underlining,
text color, background text color and strikethrough

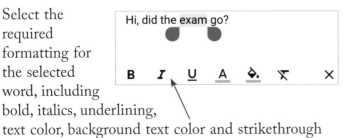

6 When you have finished composing your
email, tap on the **Send** button

Going Hands-Free

If you do not want to bother fiddling around with fingers and thumbs to create your messages, you can use speech mode instead:

1 Open a new text message or email and tap on the microphone button

2 When the **Speak now** window appears, speak your message as clearly as possible

3 As you are speaking, the **Listening...** window appears

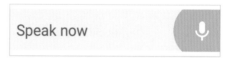

4 Your words will be converted into text

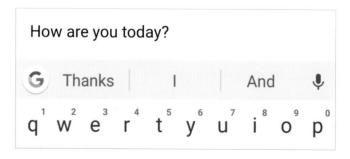

Beware

Creating text with the microphone is not an exact science and you may find that you end up with some strange interpretations of your words.

8 Android Apps

The functionality on an Android phone is provided by its apps. This chapter details the built-in ones, and shows how to download more and update them. It also looks at some of the most common apps, covering maps, notes, social media, health and fitness and games.

124 Apps for Android

126 Google Apps

128 Maps

130 Notes and Memos

131 Social Media

132 Health and Fitness

133 Playing Games

134 Around the Play Store

136 Finding Apps

138 Downloading Apps

140 Uninstalling Apps

142 Updating Apps

144 App Information

Apps for Android

An app is just a more modern name for a computer program. The terminology first became widely used on smartphones, but has now spread to all forms of computing and is firmly embedded in the language of phones.

On Android phones there are three types of apps:

- **Generic apps** – come built in on your Android phone. In general, these apps are specific to the manufacturer of the phone.

- **Google apps** – downloaded from the online Play Store. Google apps are compatible with the same apps on other Google devices. A number of these apps are also built in on a lot of Android phones.

- **Apps from other inventors** – non-Google apps, downloaded from the Play Store.

Generic apps

The types of generic apps that are available on Android phones include:

- **Calculator**. A standard calculator that also has some scientific functions, although not the range of a full scientific calculator.

Calculator

- **Calendar**. An app for storing appointments, important dates and other calendar information.

S Planner

- **Camera**. Android smartphones have at least one camera and most have two: a front-facing and back-facing one. These can be accessed from the Camera app.

Camera

- **Clock**. This can be used to view the time in different countries, and also functions as an alarm clock, a timer, and a stopwatch.

Clock

- **Contacts**. The Contacts app serves as an address book where you can enter details about your friends and family members. Calls and texts can be sent directly from the app.

Contacts

- **Email**. A lot of Android phones have a generic email app, which can be used to link to your email accounts. However, the Gmail app also serves this purpose.

Email

- **Fitness**. Health and fitness is increasingly popular on smartphones, and most Android phones have an app for measuring activity.

S Health

Don't forget

Health and fitness apps record details for areas including number of steps taken, calories consumed, heart rate, and workout activity.

- **Internet**. Although a generic Internet app is included with a lot of Android phones, the Google Chrome app is probably the best option for accessing the web.

Internet

- **Messages**. This is the generic app for sending text messages, which is done through your 3G/4G cellular network.

Messages

- **Phone**. This is the generic app for making calls (and accessing contacts for calls), video calls and sending text messages.

Phone

- **Photos**. In addition to the Camera app, some Android phones have a Photos app that can be used to view, manage, edit and share photos, and other models feature a Gallery app.

Gallery

- **Play Store**. Although this is a Google app, it is included on most Android phones so that you can access the Play Store for downloading apps, books, music, movies and magazines.

Play Store

Don't forget

In addition to the Play Store, some phone manufacturers also offer their own apps stores, although the range of apps is usually more limited.

- **Notes/Memos**. Notes and memo apps are provided on most Android phones, and they are useful for jotting down items such as shopping lists and packing lists for traveling.

Memo

- **Settings**. This contains all of the settings that can be applied to the phone so you can customize it to the way you want.

Settings

Google Apps

Most Android phones come with some Google apps already built in. If not, the apps can be downloaded from the Play Store. The Google apps for Android phones include:

- **Chrome**. Different Android phones have different types of browsers for accessing the web. The Chrome browser is the default on some phones.

Chrome

- **Docs**. This can be used to create word processing documents and keep them in cloud storage (online storage) or on your phone.

Docs

- **Drive**. This app provides online storage and backup for documents and files on your phone, stored by Google.

Drive

- **Gmail**. When you set up a Google Account you will also create a Gmail account for sending and receiving email. This app can be used for accessing and using your Gmail.

Gmail

- **Google**. This app can be used for accessing the Google Search function – still one of the best search facilities available. It can also be used for accessing the Google Feeds function, if set up.

Google

- **Google+**. This can be used with your Google Account to share content such as photos and updates with specific people.

Google+

- **Hangouts**. This is a Google social media app that can be used to chat with friends using either text or video and share photos.

Hangouts

- **Maps**. The Google Maps app is one of the best mapping apps available for finding locations and obtaining directions.

Maps

Hot tip

Messages from the Hangouts app can be replied to directly from the Notification panel, without having to first open the app.

- **Play Books**. This is the app for reading ebooks on an Android phone. It can be used to manage books in your library and also download new ones from the Play Store.

- **Play Games**. This is the app for accessing games from the Play Store and playing them on your phone.

- **Play Movies & TV**. Another app linked to the Play Store. It is used to view movies that you have bought or rented from the Play Store and to view your own personal videos.

- **Play Music**. This is the default music player that can be used to play your own music and also music content from the Play Store.

- **Play Newsstand**. This is a news app that collates stories on specific topics, or from certain publications.

- **Sheets**. This can be used to create spreadsheets and keep them in cloud storage (online storage) or on your phone.

- **Slides**. This can be used to create presentations and keep them in cloud storage (online storage) or on your phone.

- **Voice Search**. This is Google's app for searching for items by speaking. Tap on the app and then speak your search query.

- **YouTube**. This is the popular video sharing app that is now owned by Google. It can be used to view millions of videos covering most subjects imaginable.

Don't forget

Some Android phones have different apps for functions such as playing music and movies, and reading books and magazines. If this is the case, the Play apps here can still be downloaded from the Play Store.

Maps

The default maps app on Android phones is Google Maps; one of the best mapping apps on the market. It can be used to view locations, get directions and view transit details.

① Tap on the **Maps** app

② The current location is displayed (if Location is enabled under **Settings > Network connections**). Double-tap with one finger to zoom in; double-tap with two fingers to zoom out. Swipe outwards with thumb and forefinger to zoom in; pinch inwards to zoom out

③ To view other locations, type a place name, address, postcode or landmark in the Search box at the top of the window. Results are displayed as you type

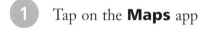

④ Tap on one of the results to view a map of it. Some locations also have additional features such as photos. Tap on an item to view it, or swipe up from the bottom of the window to view more details about a location

When viewing a map in Step 2, tap on this button to tilt the perspective of the map.

Tap on this button to return to the default view.

Tap on these buttons at the bottom of the map window to, from left to right, view information about the current location, view driving conditions for the location, view transit details, and access different layers for the map (see tip on next page).

Getting directions

The Maps app is very effective in providing directions between two points. To do this:

1   Tap on the **Go** button

2   Enter the starting point and destination for the directions in the text fields at the top of the window (by default, the starting point is your current location but this can be changed by tapping in the field and entering a new location for the starting point). The route is displayed on the map. Tap the **Menu** button to add a stop, and for more options

3   Tap on these buttons to select the mode of transport for the journey

4   Tap on the **Start** button to view step-by-step directions for the journey

5   As you change your location the map updates accordingly and gives you spoken directions. Tap the speaker button for options to turn off spoken directions (mute) or to hear alerts only

Tap on the **Menu** button on the bottom toolbar, when viewing a location on a map, to access the **Map layers** option. This can be used to view different overlays for the map, including bicycle routes, satellite view which shows the map as a photo and terrain view which shows the contours of hills and mountains.

Notes and Memos

Taking notes on an Android phone is an excellent way to keep up-to-date with a range of tasks, from shopping lists to reminders for packing for a trip. There are several notes and memos apps that can be downloaded from the Play Store, and most smartphone manufacturers include a default notes and memos app The example here uses the Samsung Memo app. To use it:

1 Tap on the **Memo** app

2 Tap on this button to create a new memo

3 Enter a title for the memo and the text for the memo

Hot tip

When creating a new memo or note, tap on these buttons at the top of the window to, from left to right, add a new category for memos, add photos, or record a voice memo.

Some Android phone models include text editing features, checkboxes and using a pen to draw directly onto the note.

4 Once the memo is completed, tap on the **Save** button

5 The memo is added to the **My memos** homepage

6 Each time a new memo is added, it is listed at the top of the My memos page. Tap on a memo to view it and edit it, if required

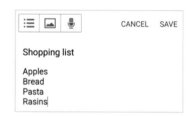
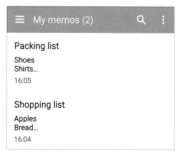

Social Media

Social media has transformed the way in which we communicate and there are numerous apps that can be used on an Android phone for social media. These can be downloaded from the **Play Store**, from within the **Social** category. Some of the most popular apps are:

Facebook

This is still one of the most widely-used social media tools. To use Facebook you have to first register, which is free. You can then link up with your friends and share a variety of content, by searching for them and inviting them to join your network with a Friend Request.

Twitter

Twitter is a microblogging site where users post short messages (tweets). Once you have joined Twitter, which is free, you can follow other users to see what they are saying and have people follow you too.

Snapchat

Snapchat is a messaging service that allows users to send photos and videos to their Snapchat friends, or groups of people. Once these are accessed, they remain visible for a few seconds and then they are deleted. Text and graphics can be added to items when they are sent – one of the most frequent uses is for sending self-portraits ("selfies" – see page 162).

Pinterest

This is an online pinboard, where you can bookmark and "pin" items of interest, and upload your own content for other people to pin.

Instagram

This is a popular photo and video sharing site. Followers can be added by users and they can then comment and "like" photos. By default, the security settings are for public viewing of content, so these should be changed if you only want your own followers to be able to view your content.

Google+ is a social networking app that is similar to Facebook in terms of creating online communities for sharing content.

YouTube is one of the great successes of the internet age. It is a video sharing site, with millions of video clips covering every subject imaginable. There is a built-in YouTube app on most Android phones, which can be accessed from the All Apps button.

The Google Fit app can be downloaded from the Play Store, as can a range of health and fitness apps.

Hot tip

Tap on the **Add activity** button in Step 3 to manually add details of an activity that has not been recorded by the app on the phone.

132

Don't forget

Once an activity has been paused as in Step 5, tap on the **Play** button (below, left) to restart it, or the **Stop** button (below, right) to save the activity details within the app.

Health and Fitness

Wearable fitness devices have enjoyed great success in recent years: they can be used to monitor health and fitness, and also record exercise and workout information. Individual devices have their own specific apps for recording items, but there is also a range of health and fitness apps that can record exercise activity on your Android phone. The default one is the Google Fit app. To use this:

1. Tap on the **Fit** app

2. Tap on this button to enter health and fitness information or start a new activity

3. Select an option from the menu, e.g. **Start activity**

   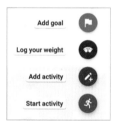

4. Select the type of activity that you want to perform, and tap on the **Start** button

   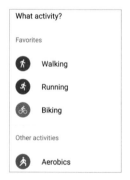

5. The details of the activity are recorded, including distance covered (if applicable), number or steps and calories used. Tap on the **Pause** button to pause the session

Playing Games

Although computer games may seem like the preserve of the younger generation, this is definitely not the case. Not all computer games are of the shoot-em-up or racing variety, and the Play Store also contains puzzles and versions of popular board games. Some games to try are:

- **Chess**. Pit your wits against this Chess app. Various settings can be applied for each game, such as the level of difficulty.

- **Checkers**. Similar to the Chess app, but for Checkers (Draughts). Hints are also available to help develop your skills and knowledge.

- **Mahjong**. A version of the popular Chinese game, this is a matching game for single players, rather than playing with other people.

- **Scrabble**. An Android phone version of the best-selling word game that can be played with up to four people.

- **Solitaire**. An old favorite, the card game where you have to build sequences and remove all of the cards.

- **Sudoku**. The logic game where you have to fill different grids with numbers 1-9, without having any of the same number in a row or column.

- **Tetris**. One of the original computer games, where you have to piece together falling shapes to make lines.

- **Words With Friends**. Similar to Scrabble, an online word game, played with other users.

Don't forget

As well as the games here, there is a full range of other types of games in the Play Store, which can be accessed from the **Games** category. They can also be accessed from the **Play Games** app.

Play Games

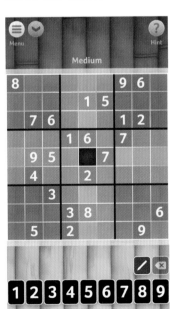

Around the Play Store

Although the built-in apps provide a lot of useful functionality and are a good starting point, the Play Store is where you can really start to take advantage of the wide range of apps that are available. These can be used for entertainment, communication, productivity and much more.

To access the Play Store and find apps:

New apps are added to the Play Store on a regular basis (and existing ones are updated), so the Homepage will change appearance regularly.

1 Tap on the **Play Store** app

2 Suggested items are shown on the Play Store Homepage

134

App prices are shown in the local currency.

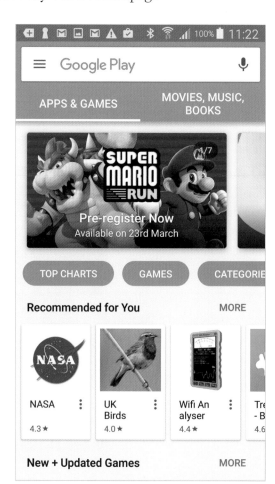

3 Swipe up and down or left and right to see the full range of recommendations for all types of content in the Play Store. Tap on an item to view further details about it

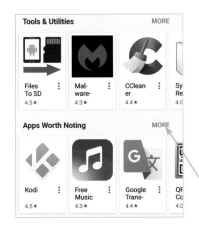

Tap on the **More** button from a section on the Homepage to view additional items.

MORE

4 Use these buttons to find relevant content: **Apps & Games** or **Movies, Music, Books**

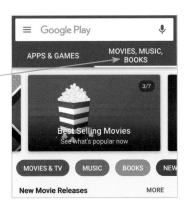

135

5 Tap on the **Menu** button to access the Play Store menu

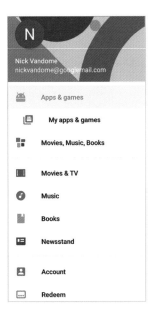

If you have a Play Store Gift Card, it can be redeemed from the **Redeem** button at the bottom of the menu in Step 5. Enter the Gift Card code, and the relevant amount will be credited to your Google Play balance for use in the Play Store.

Finding Apps

Searching by category

When you have accessed the Play Store you can then look for content in a variety of ways:

There may be different apps available in the Play Store depending on your geographical location.

1 The featured and recommended items are displayed on the Apps Homepage. Swipe up and down and left and right to view the full range and tap on an item to view more details

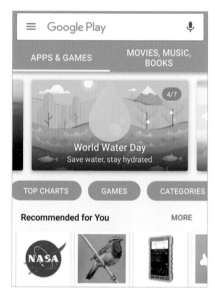

2 Swipe left and right on the top bar to view apps according to **Top Charts**, **Games**, **Categories**, **Family**, **Editors' Choice** and **Early Access**

...cont'd

3 Tap on the **Categories** tab in Step 2 and tap on a category to view the apps according to the relevant headings

CATEGORIES

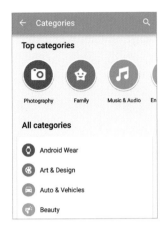

4 Search for apps within a category in the same way as for searching over the whole range of apps, as in Step 2

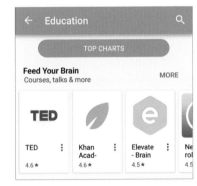

Using the Search box

1 Tap in the Play Store Search box on any page to conduct a search with keywords

≡ Google Play

2 Enter the name of the item for which you want to search

3 Tap on one of the suggested results, or tap on this button on the keyboard to conduct another search

As you type in the Search box, the suggested items will change, depending on the keyword(s) used.

Downloading Apps

Once you have found an app in the Play Store that you want to use, you can download it to your phone:

Hot tip

If you have a phone with 3G/4G cellular capability, try downloading apps over Wi-Fi to avoid using too much of your data allowance.

Don't forget

If an app has a Price button on it, you will need to add credit/debit card details to your Google Account. This can be done when the account is set up, or from the Play Store menu (**Account > Payment methods**).

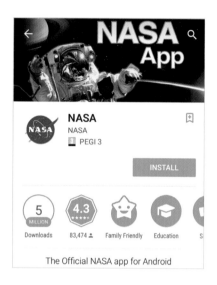

Hot tip

Under **Settings > Applications > Application settings** select apps to apply settings for their notifications in the Notification panel.

1 Access the app you want to use. There will be details about the app and reviews from other users if you scroll down the page

2 Tap on the **Install** button, and the app will start downloading

INSTALL

3 Tap on the **Open** button to open the app once it has finished downloading and installing

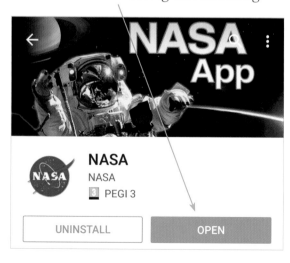

4 Some apps require the user to accept their terms and conditions of usage. Tap on the **Accept** button to accept and continue using the app

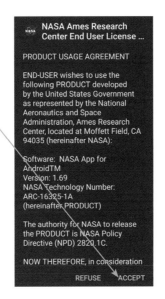

5 Some apps will also request permission for items such as accessing your location. **Allow** or **Deny** as required

Allow **NASA** to access this device's location?

DENY   ALLOW

Don't forget

If an app has access to your device's location it creates more location-specific content. If you deny an app permissions, it may not work.

6 Newly downloaded apps usually appear on the next available All Apps screen where there is a space. From here, the app can be opened and also moved to another location. A shortcut on your Home screen is sometimes also created

Uninstalling Apps

The built-in apps on an Android phone cannot be deleted easily (although they can be turned off), but the ones that have been downloaded from the Play Store can be uninstalled. You may want to do this if you do not use a certain app any more, or you feel the number of apps on your phone is becoming unmanageable. To uninstall a downloaded app:

Don't forget

If apps are selected in the same way as in Step 1 from any Home screen, the available button is **Remove**. Drag the app over the **Remove** button to remove it from the Home screen, but it will still be available from the All Apps section. Built-in apps cannot be uninstalled, but they can be removed from the Home screen.

Don't forget

If apps have been uninstalled from the phone, they can be reinstalled from the Play Store app by selecting **My apps & games** from the main menu and tapping on the **Library** option to view all of the apps that have previously been downloaded.

① Access the **All Apps** section and press and hold on one of the apps until the **Uninstall** button appears

② Drag the app over the **Uninstall** button until it turns red, and release to uninstall the app

③ Tap on the **OK** button to confirm the uninstall

NASA

Do you want to uninstall this app?

CANCEL   OK

...cont'd

Turning off built-in apps

Built-in apps cannot be uninstalled easily, but they can be
turned off so that they cannot be used. This is done from the
All Apps area, in a similar way for uninstalling apps:

1 Press and hold the app to be turned off.
The button on the top toolbar is now
Turn off rather than Uninstall. Drag
the app over here to turn it off

2 A warning will appear
alerting you to the fact
that you are disabling the
app. Tap on the **Turn Off**
button to continue

Disable app

Play Newsstand and all related features will be disabled.
To enable Play Newsstand
again, go to Settings >
Application manager.

CANCEL   TURN OFF

Phone manufacturers
can add their own
apps to Android
phones and, in some
cases, it is not possible
to either uninstall or
turn off these apps.

141

3 To turn the app
back on, access
**Settings >
Applications
> Application
manager** and
tap on the turned off app

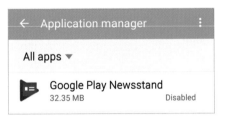

← Application manager

All apps ▼

Google Play Newsstand
32.35 MB   Disabled

4 Tap on the
Enable button
to turn the app
back on again

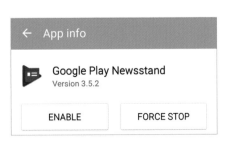

← App info

Google Play Newsstand
Version 3.5.2

ENABLE   FORCE STOP

Updating Apps

The world of apps is a dynamic and fast-moving one, and new apps are being created and added to the Play Store on a daily basis. Existing apps are also being updated, to improve their performance and functionality. These can be added to your phone either automatically or manually:

Updating apps automatically

Hot tip

Apps are also updated to improve security features and include any fixes to improve the performance of the app.

Hot tip

Some app updates will require your confirmation before updating, even if you have chosen to auto-update apps.

1 Access the Play Store. Tap on the **Menu** button and then the **Settings** button

Settings

2 Tap on the **Auto-update apps** option

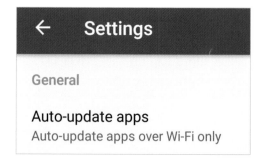

← **Settings**

General

Auto-update apps
Auto-update apps over Wi-Fi only

3 Tap on the **Auto-update apps over Wi-Fi only** radio button so that it contains a green dot. Available updates will be installed

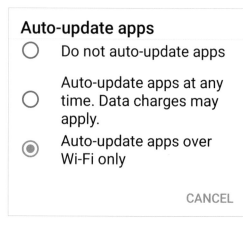

Auto-update apps

○ Do not auto-update apps

○ Auto-update apps at any time. Data charges may apply.

◉ Auto-update apps over Wi-Fi only

CANCEL

automatically when the phone is connected to Wi-Fi

Updating apps manually
Apps can also be updated manually:

1 Ensure **Do not auto-update apps** is selected in Step 3 on the previous page

2 Access the Play Store. Tap on the **Menu** button and then the **My apps & games** option

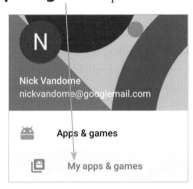

If apps are set to be updated manually, check regularly in the Play Store to see if there are any updates that you want to install for your apps.

143

3 Tap on the **Installed** tab to view the apps on your phone. Select the **Updates** tab and then tap here to update all of the appropriate apps, or tap on the **Update** button next to a specific app to update it

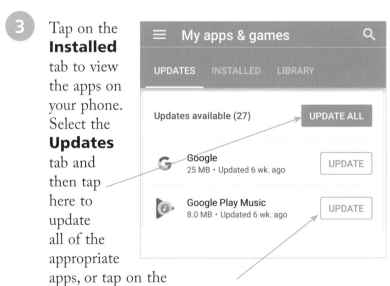

App Information

For both built-in apps and those downloaded from the Play Store, it is possible to view details about them and also see the permissions that they are using to access certain functions. To view information about your apps:

1 Open the **Settings** app and tap on the **Application manager** button under the **Applications** section

Application manager

2 Tap on an app to select it and view its details

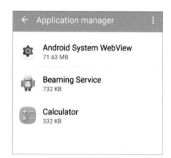

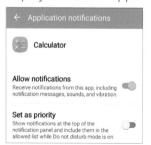
Tap on the **Notifications** button in the **App info** window to specify how notifications are handled for the app. Drag the **Allow notifications** button to **On** to enable notifications to be displayed for the app.

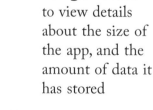

3 Tap on the **Force Stop** button to close a running app

4 Tap on the **Data usage** button to view details about the size of the app, and the amount of data it has stored

5 Tap on the **Permissions** button to view what the app is accessing on your phone (if anything)

9 Being Entertained

Android phones are not only useful, they are also great fun. This chapter shows how to make the most of your phone and use it for playing music, watching movies and reading books.

146 The Google Play Website

147 Music on Android

148 Downloading Music

150 Playing Music

153 Managing Music

154 Pinning Music

156 Movies and TV Shows

158 Obtaining Ebooks

160 Around an Ebook

The Google Play Website

Google Play is Google's online store for buying, downloading, using and managing a range of entertainment content. It is accessed at the website:

- **play.google.com**

You need to have a Google Account in order to log in to the Google Play website. Once you have logged in to Google Play you can download a variety of content:

For details about accessing websites, see page 175.

Content that is downloaded to your Android phone via the Play Store will also be available on the Google Play website, as long as you are logged in with your Google Account.

If you buy music from either the Play Store or the Google Play website, it can be played on your phone with streaming (using a Wi-Fi internet connection – see page 150) or it can be downloaded (pinned) onto your phone so that you can also listen to it offline (see pages 154-155).

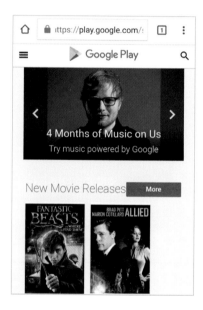

- Music

- Movies and TV shows

- Apps

- Ebooks

Content from Google Play is stored in the cloud so it can then be used on your computer and also your Android phone. If you delete it from your phone, either accidentally or on purpose, you can still reinstall it from Google Play. You can also use content downloaded by any of your other Android devices, such as a tablet.

Music on Android

One option for playing music on an Android phone is the Google Play Music app. It can be used to play music that has been obtained in a number of different ways:

Play Music

- Downloaded directly to your phone from the **Play Store**.

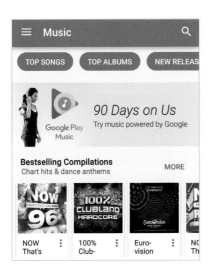

- Bought on **Google Play** and then used on another device.

- Transferred from your computer directly to your phone. This is done by connecting your phone to your computer, using the USB cable, and copying your music to the **Music** folder on your phone, and then locating the music files through the Play Music app.

- Transferred from another mobile device using Bluetooth.

Don't forget

Google Play Music also offers a subscription service that enables users to download unlimited music through the Play Music app or the Google Play Store. There is a standard 30 day free trial (some phone manufacturers offer a longer free trial of Play Music), with options for either Individual or Family memberships after the free period finishes. Google Play Music can be joined when you first open the Play Music app.

Downloading Music

To use your phone directly to find and download music from the Play Store:

In some cases, there may be sample content in the Play Music app to help you get started with playing music.

1 Tap on the **Play Music** app to open the music player

Play Music

2 Tap on the **Menu** button to access the Play Music menu, and tap on the **Shop** button

Music library

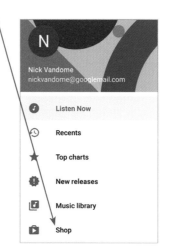

N

Nick Vandome
nickvandome@googlemail.com

♪ Listen Now

⏱ Recents

★ Top charts

✦ New releases

▣ Music library

▶ Shop

3 Use these buttons to view the relevant sections within the Music section of the Play Store, or

4 Tap on these sections to view the recommended content, or

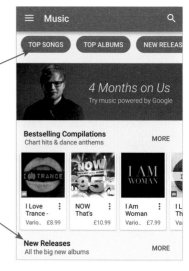

≡ Music 🔍

TOP SONGS TOP ALBUMS NEW RELEAS

4 Months on Us
Try music powered by Google

Bestselling Compilations
Chart hits & dance anthems MORE

I Love ⋮ NOW ⋮ I Am ⋮ I L
Trance - That's Woman Th
Vario.. £8.99 £10.99 Vario.. £7.99 Va

New Releases
All the big new albums MORE

5 Tap on this button and enter an artist, album or song name into the Search box

6 Locate the item you want to download. For an album, tap on this button to buy the full album, or swipe up the page and tap on the price button next to an individual song

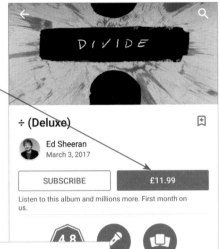

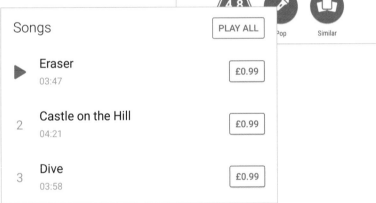

When you buy music from the Play Store it also comes with the related artwork such as album or singles covers.

7 Tap on the **Buy** button and enter your Google Account password to buy the item and download it to your phone

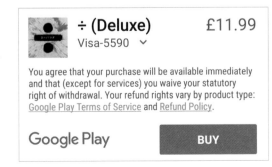

Playing Music

Once you have obtained music on your phone, by whatever means, you can then start playing it and listening to it. To do this:

1 Tap on the **Play Music** app

Play Music

2 All of the available music is displayed. This includes music from the Play Music store that is only available for streaming at this point, i.e. it needs a Wi-Fi connection to play it

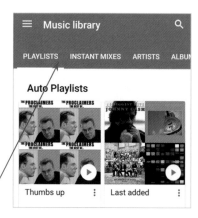

3 Tap on these buttons to view your music content according to **Playlists**, **Instant Mixes**, **Artists**, **Albums**, **Songs** and **Genres**

4 Tap on an item to view the available songs (for an album) or individual tracks

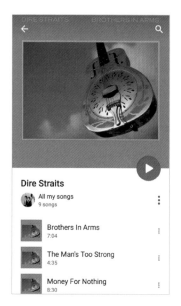

5 Tap on a song to play it. The currently-playing song is also displayed at the bottom of the Play Music app

6 Tap on the song or album icon to view the song artwork at full size, and view the standard playback controls at the bottom of the window

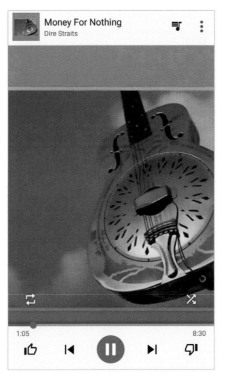

Hot tip

Invest in a reasonable set of headphones to listen to music on your Android phone. This will usually result in a higher quality sound than through the built-in speakers.

151

7 When a song is playing, this button appears next to it

...cont'd

Music controls

When a song is playing there are several options:

1 Use these buttons to, from left to right, go back to the beginning of a song, Pause/Play a song, 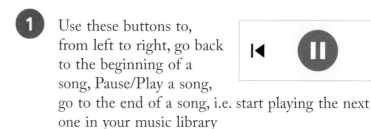 go to the end of a song, i.e. start playing the next one in your music library

2 For an album, tap on this button to view the current queue of songs

3 The full range of music controls appears at the bottom of the screen

4 Drag this button to move through a song

5 Tap on this button to shuffle the songs in your collection

6 Tap on this button to loop the currently-queued songs

7 For music purchased from the Google Play Store, you can tap on these buttons to rate the song

Don't forget

Queued songs are those waiting to be played in the Play Music app.

Hot tip

Music controls can also be accessed from the Google Play Music Widget, the Lock screen when music is playing, and the Notification panel when music is playing.

Managing Music

When you are playing music there is still a certain amount of flexibility in terms of managing what is playing, and being scheduled to play. This is known as the music queue. To use this to manage your music:

1 Tap on this button next to an album or a song

2 Tap on the **Add to queue** button to add it to the current queue of songs

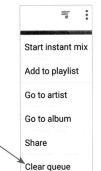

3 View the song queue as shown in Step 2 on the previous page, and tap on this button again to hide it

4 When viewing the current queue, tap on the **Menu** button

5 Tap on the **Clear queue** button to remove all of the songs from the current queue

6 When viewing the songs in the queue, tap on the same button as in Step 1 and make one of the related selections, including **Remove from queue**

Hot tip

When viewing the current queue, press and hold on the bar to the left of the song title and drag it to reorder its position in the current queue.

Beware

If you select **Clear queue**, this closes the currently-playing item. However, it does not remove it from your phone and it remains available in the Play Music app.

Pinning Music

Music that is bought from the Google Play Store is available for streaming on your phone using your Wi-Fi internet connection. This means that the music is sent from the Google servers, where it is stored. This means that it is always backed up and always available.

However, if you are not able to use Wi-Fi, you will probably still want to listen to your music, such as when you are traveling. This can be done by pinning the required music to your phone so that it is physically stored there. To do this:

Beware

Items that are not pinned to your device will not be available when you do not have a Wi-Fi connection.

1 Access the Play Music Menu and toggle **On** or **Off** the **Downloaded only** button to view the music on your phone that has already been downloaded to it, rather than just being stored within the Google cloud (i.e. the servers that keep the music that you have bought)

| Downloaded only | ⬜ |

| Downloaded only | 🔘 |

2 For **Downloaded only**, the items that are stored on your phone are shown

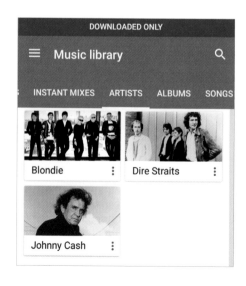

3 The icons next to an item denote its status according to whether it is downloaded to the device or not. A grayed-out button indicates an item that has been bought from the Google Play Store but has not been downloaded to the device. An orange button with a white tick indicates that an item has been downloaded to your phone, i.e. pinned

4 Tap on a grayed-out button so that the pin turns orange, to start the process for downloading and then pinning the item to your phone

Beware

The more music that you download to your phone, the more storage space it will take up.

5 The item will be downloaded for storing on your phone. This is indicated in the Notifications bar by the arrow icon

6 Swipe down on the Notifications bar to see the progress of the track(s) being downloaded

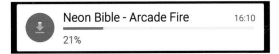

Neon Bible - Arcade Fire   16:10
21%

Beware

Downloading items over 3G/4G can be expensive.

7 Tap on an item in Step 6 to view the full download queue

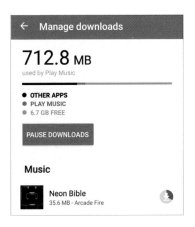

← Manage downloads

712.8 MB
used by Play Music

● OTHER APPS
● PLAY MUSIC
● 6.7 GB FREE

PAUSE DOWNLOADS

Music

Neon Bible
35.6 MB - Arcade Fire

Movies and TV Shows

There are different ways in which video content can be viewed on your Android phone:

- Downloading movies and TV shows from the Google Play Store.

- Transferring (uploading) to, or creating your own videos on your phone.

- Watching videos on YouTube.

To obtain movies or TV shows from the Play Store:

Some phones have their own default movies app, which will be linked to the phone manufacturer's own app store. If this is the case, the Play Movies app can still be downloaded from the Play Store, and content can be bought from there.

1 Tap on the **Play Movies & TV** app

2 Tap here and then tap on the **Library** button to view available content on your phone. This includes movies and TV shows that you have downloaded, and also recommended titles

When buying or renting items from the Play Store, there are usually options for doing so in Standard Definition (SD) or High Definition (HD).

3 Tap on an item in the **Library** section to view it

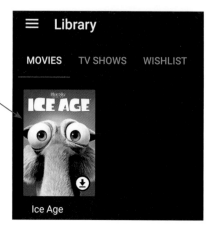

4 Tap on the **Shop** button in Step 2 to view the available movies and TV shows in the Play Store

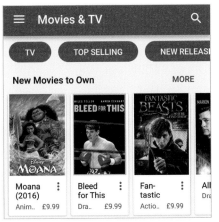

5 The **Movies & TV** section of the Play Store is similar to those for the other types of content

6 Tap on the main panels to view highlighted or recommended movies and TV shows

7 Tap on an item to view details about it. Tap here to watch a preview clip of the item

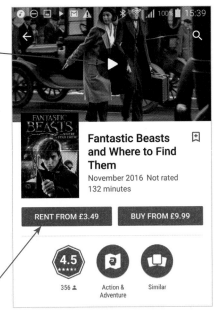

8 Tap on these buttons to buy or rent a movie or TV show. This will be made available within the Play Movies app. (If you rent a movie or a TV show it has to be started within 30 days of being rented, and watched within 48 hours of when it was first started)

Don't forget

Tap the **Genres** button at the top of the Movies & TV window to view the different categories. These include Action & Adventure, Animation, Comedy, Documentary, Drama, Family, Horror, Romance, Sci-Fi and Thriller.

157

Beware

If you download movies and TV shows to your phone, they can take up a considerable amount of storage space. Rented items will be automatically deleted once the rental period expires.

Obtaining Ebooks

Due to their size and portability, Android phones are often used for reading ebooks. There is a wide range that can be downloaded from the Play Store, or from the Google Play website, in a similar way to obtaining music, movies and apps.

Don't forget

Android phones with larger screens are recommended for reading ebooks.

Don't forget

Swipe left and right on a panel on the Books Homepage to view the items within it.

Hot tip

The Kindle app can be downloaded from the Play Store for reading ebooks. If you already have a Kindle account, your ebooks will be available through the Kindle app on your phone.

1 Tap on the **Play Books** app (or access the Google Play website)

Play Books

2 Any ebooks that you already have on your phone will be displayed in the **Library** section. Tap on a cover to open a specific title

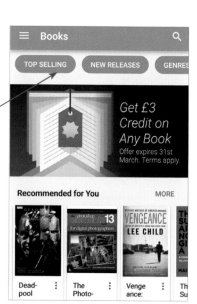

3 Tap on the **Menu** button and tap on the **Shop** button

4 Ebooks can be browsed for and downloaded in a similar way as for other Play Store content. Tap on these buttons to view ebooks according to these headings

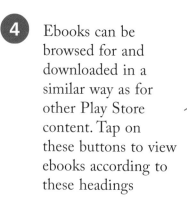

5 Tap on a title to view details about it

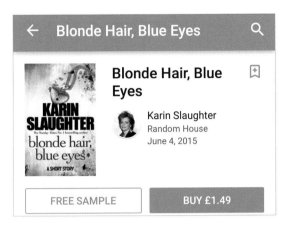

6 When you find an ebook you want to read, tap on the **Free Sample** button (if there is one) or the **Buy** button (with the price)

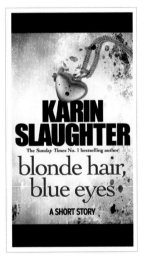

7 When any ebook from the Play Books store has been downloaded to your phone, it is available within your Play Books library

8 Simply select it to open it, and tap in the middle of the page to access the reading controls

One of the categories in the Play Store Books section is for **Top Free** ebooks. Some classic titles also have free versions if the copyright has expired after a certain period of time following the author's death.

Check out the ebook version of this title and other **In Easy Steps** ebooks in the Play Store. Samples for all titles are downloadable for free:

Around an Ebook

Once you have downloaded ebooks to your phone, you can start reading them. Due to their format there is a certain amount of electronic functionality that is not available in a hard copy version. To find your way around an ebook:

Don't forget

You can also move to the next or previous page by tapping at the right-hand or left-hand edge of a page.

1 Swipe left and right on a page to move backwards or forwards by one page

2 Tap in the middle of a page to access the reading controls toolbars at the top and bottom of the screen

Search inside   Font size and settings

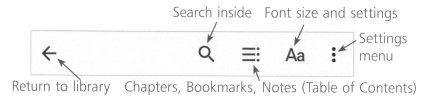

Settings menu

Return to library   Chapters, Bookmarks, Notes (Table of Contents)

Hot tip

To delete an ebook from the Play Books app, in your library, tap on this button below the ebook cover and tap on the **Delete from library** option. The ebook can be reinstalled from the Play Store if you want to place it in your library again. This is free to do.

3 Drag this button to move through the ebook

4 Tap on this button to access the ebook's Table of Contents, bookmarks and notes

5 Tap on the **Menu** button to access the specific settings for the title you are reading

6 Tap on this button to select text options including font size and line height

Buy

Remove download

Delete from library

Buy as gift

About this book

7 Tap in the top right-hand corner of a page to add a bookmark. A blue bookmark icon appears. Tap again to remove it. Tap on the button in Step 4 to view all bookmarks

Monday, March 4, 1991

7:26 am – North Lumpkin Street, Athens, Georgia

The morning mist laced through the downtown streets,

10 Keeping in the Picture

This chapter shows how to make the most of the high-quality cameras that come with most Android phones.

162 Using Cameras

164 Adding Photos

166 Viewing Photos

169 Adding Folders

170 Editing Photos

172 Sharing Photos

Using Cameras

Most Android phones have their own built in cameras, which can be used to capture photos directly onto the device. The quality of these varies between makes of phone. Some are good quality cameras intended to be used for taking photos in a range of conditions; others are mainly for use as a webcam for video calls, or for "selfies" (these are front-facing cameras). To use an Android camera phone:

Hot tip

Use the front-facing camera, i.e. the one on the phone's screen, to take "selfies" which are self-portraits, which can also include other people.

1. Tap on the **Camera** app

2. The Camera app displays the current scene, and the control buttons are displayed at the side (landscape view) or at the bottom (portrait view)

Don't forget

The most recently captured photo is displayed at the left-hand side of the bottom toolbar. Tap on it to open it in the Photos app.

3. Press on the screen to focus the current scene and tap on this button to take a photo

4. Further controls are available at the top of the screen on the shortcuts bar

Don't forget

Tap on the **Video** button in Step 2 to record a video rather than take a photo.

5. Tap on this button to switch between the front- and rear-facing cameras

...cont'd

6 Tap on the **Settings** button to view the full range of settings for the camera

7 Tap on one of the items to activate or deactivate it, e.g. the camera's flash functionality

8 For the most-used functions, drag the icon to the top shortcuts bar so that it can be accessed from there

9 Tap on the **Mode** button on the bottom toolbar to view the camera's different shooting modes

10 Tap on one of the shooting modes to select that for the next photo. Auto is the default mode, but there are a range of other alternatives, including Panorama and portrait mode (Beauty face)

Don't forget

By default, photos captured with the Camera are displayed in the **Photos** or **Gallery** app.

Don't forget

Different models of Android phones have their own cameras, which include specific settings and modes. However, the ones listed here will be similar across most Android cameras.

163

Adding Photos

Android phones are great for storing and, more importantly, displaying your photos. The screen size of most phones is ideal for looking at photos and you can quickly transform it into your own mobile photo album. In addition, it is also possible to share all of your photos in a variety of ways.

Obtaining photos

In addition to capturing photos with your phone, you can obtain them in a number of ways:

- Transferring photos from your computer directly to your phone, via a USB cable (into the **Pictures** folder).

- Transferring photos from your camera to your phone. This is usually done by inserting your camera's memory card into a card reader connected to your computer and then transferring your photos.

- Downloading and saving photos from an email, social media, website or from an internet messaging app.

- Transferring photos from another device via Bluetooth.

Once you have captured or transferred photos to your phone you can then view, edit and share them using the **Photos** app. Photos in the Photos app are stored in different albums, which are created automatically when photos are taken, transferred, or downloaded from an email.

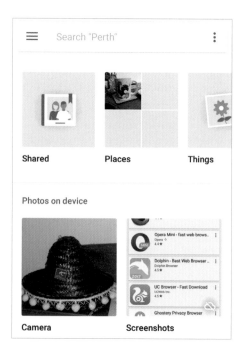

Beware

If you keep a lot of photos on your phone this will start to take up its storage space.

Hot tip

Personal videos can also be transferred in the same way as with photos. Copy them into the **Videos** folder of your phone. Videos can also be recorded with the video button in the Camera app.

Downloading from email

Email is a good method of obtaining photos on your phone; other people can send their photos to you in this way, and you can also email your own photos from a computer, a tablet or another mobile device. To use photos from email:

1 Open the email containing the photo and tap on this button to download it

Don't forget

Once the **Download** folder has been created, all other photos downloaded from emails will be placed here.

165

2 The photo will be saved in the **Download** folder within the **Photos** app. This will be automatically created if it is not already there

3 Tap on the photo to open the album, and tap on it again to view it at full size in the Photos app

Viewing Photos

Once you have obtained photos on your Android phone you can start viewing, managing and editing them.

1 Open the **Photos** app and tap on the **Menu** button at the top of the Photos window to view the options

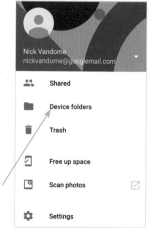

2 Tap on the **Device folders** button from the menu

Don't forget

The default albums in the Photos app are initially empty.

3 Tap on the **Albums** button at the bottom of the screen to view the available albums

Albums

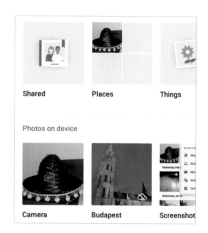

4 Tap on the **Photos** button at the bottom of the screen to view photos that have been taken with the phone's camera

Photos

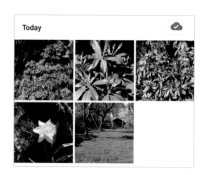

...cont'd

The photos in the Photos app can be worked with and viewed in different ways:

1 Open the **Photos** app and access the **Photos** section as shown on the previous page

2 The photos and the date on which they were taken are displayed. Tap on a photo to view it at full size

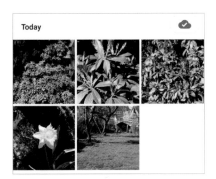

3 In the main window, tap on the **Menu** button and tap on the **Select...** button to select individual photos

4 Use the **Menu** button to view the options for working with the images in the folder. This includes selecting items, changing the layout format on the screen to Day, Month or Year view, or creating new items such as a new album

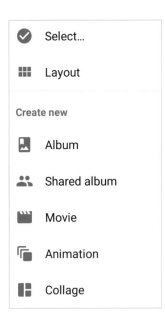

Hot tip

You can also press and hold on photos to select them.

Don't forget

The **Layout** of photos can be in Day, Month or Year view.

...cont'd

Hot tip

Items selected in Step 5 can be shared in a variety of ways by tapping on this button (see page 172 for details).

5 To select items, click on the **Select...** button in Step 4 on the previous page and tap on the items you want to select, denoted by a blue circle with a white tick

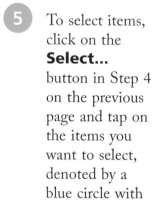

6 Tap on a photo to view it at full size. Tap on this button to access the photo's menu options, or use the bottom toolbar buttons to share, edit, view information, or delete the photo

7 Select options from the photo's menu, including creating a slideshow, adding the photo to an album, using it as a contact photo or wallpaper image, printing the photo, editing the photo or deleting it from the device

Slideshow
Add to album
Use as
Print
Edit in
Delete device copy

Adding Folders

In addition to the pre-inserted device folders, new ones can be added either from the Photos or the Albums section of the Photos app. To do this:

1 Tap on the **Menu** button

2 Tap on the **Album** button under the **Create new** heading

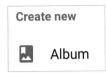

3 Tap on the photos to be included in the album and tap on the **Create** button

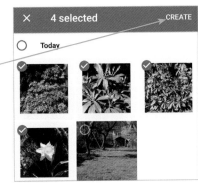

4 Tap here and give the album a name, then tap on the tick symbol

5 The new album is included in the **Albums** section

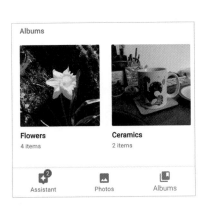

Hot tip

Individual photos can be added to albums by viewing them at full size, tapping on the **Menu** button as in Step 6 on the previous page, tapping on the **Add to album** button and selecting the required album. Alternatively, select them as in Step 5 on the previous page, click the **+** (plus) button, and select **New album**.

Editing Photos

Although the Photos app is more for viewing photos, it does have a few editing options so that you can tweak and enhance your images. To access and use these:

1 Tap on a photo to view it. Tap on this button to access the editing options

2 Tap on this button on the bottom toolbar to access the filter options. Tap on one of the filters to apply it to the photo

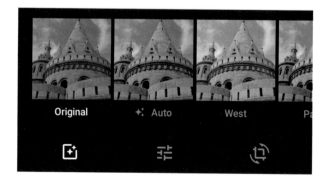

3 Tap on this button to select a range of color editing functions, including editing 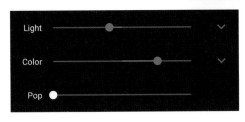 the brightness and color contrast of the photo. Drag the sliders to change the effect

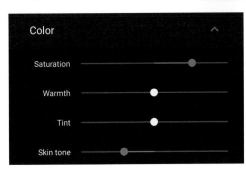

4 Tap on this button next to one of the color editing options to expand it and access sliders for editing elements within the main category

5 To crop a photo, tap on the **Crop** button and drag the resizing handles as required

6 Tap on this button to **Rotate** the photo manually, clockwise or anticlockwise. Tap on the **Done** button to finish editing

7 Tap on the **Save** button to save any editing changes that have been made

Hot tip

Most photos benefit from some cropping, to give the main subject more prominence.

Sharing Photos

It can be great fun and very rewarding to share photos with friends and family. With an Android phone this can be done in several ways:

Social networking sites such as Facebook and Twitter are ideal for sharing photos. Their respective apps can be downloaded from the Play Store, in which case they will also appear as one of the sharing options in Step 2.

Beware

If you are sending photos by Bluetooth, the other device must be paired with your phone, have Bluetooth turned on and accept the request to download the photos when they are sent. When pairing two devices, a password will be created on the first device that then needs to be entered into the second device.

1 Select an album or open an individual photo and tap on the **Share** button

2 Select one of the sharing options. This will be dependent on the apps on your phone, but should include email, messaging and online storage options such as Google Drive

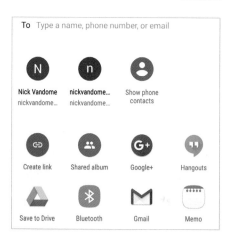

Sharing with Bluetooth

To share with another device with Bluetooth:

1 Access a photo or make a selection of photos (as shown in Step 5 on page 168), tap on the **Share** button, and then the **Bluetooth** option in Step 2 above

Bluetooth

2 If your Bluetooth is not on, tap on the **Turn on** button to activate it

3 Select the device with which you want to share your photo(s). These will be sent wirelessly via Bluetooth

11 Online with Chrome

This chapter looks at browser options on Android and also viewing all of your favorite websites with the Chrome browser.

174 Android Web Browsers

175 Opening Pages

176 Bookmarking Pages

178 Links and Images

179 Using Tabs

180 Being Incognito

181 Browser Settings

Don't forget

Mobile versions of a website usually have **m.** before the rest of the website address, e.g. **m.mysite.com**

Android Web Browsers

Web browsing is an essential part of our digital world, and on Android phones this functionality can be provided by a variety of web browsers customized for this purpose. They can usually display websites in two ways:

● Optimized for viewing on mobile devices, which are versions that are designed specifically for viewing in this format.

● Full versions of websites (rather than the mobile versions), which are the same as used on a desktop computer.

Different Android phones have different default browsers but they all have the same general functionality:

● Viewing web pages.

● Bookmarking pages.

● Tabbed browsing, i.e. using tabs to view more than one web page within the same browser window.

If you do not want to use the default browser that is provided with your phone, there is a range of browsers that can be downloaded, for free, from the Play Store.

Enter **browsers for android** into the **Play Store Search box** to view the available options.

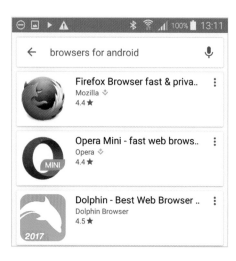

Opening Pages

Web pages can be opened on a phone in an almost identical way as on a desktop computer or laptop. Some Android web browsers display a list of top sites when you open a browser or create a new tab. (The examples on the following pages are for the **Chrome** browser but other browsers operate in a similar way.)

1 The **Search/Address** box can be used to search for keywords or phrases, or you can use it to find specific web pages and sites. Enter text into the **Search/Address** box. If a web address is displayed, tap on it to go directly to that website

2 Tap on the arrow next to an item to select it in the **Search/Address** box. Tap on the item in the **Search/Address** box to view it

3 For a web address, e.g. one that ends in .com, the web page will be opened; if you have just entered a keyword in the Search/Address box, then the results page will be opened for that keyword. Tap one of the links as required

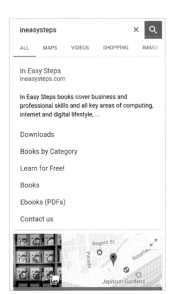

The Chrome browser can be downloaded from the Play Store if it is not already on your phone. This is a Google product and integrates closely with other Google apps on your phone.

175

Swipe outwards with your thumb and forefinger on a web page to zoom in on it; pinch inwards to zoom back out. You can double-tap with one finger to zoom in and out too, but this zooms in to a lesser degree than swiping.

Bookmarking Pages

The favorite web pages that you visit can be bookmarked so that you can find them quickly. To do this:

1 Open the page that you want to bookmark and tap on the **Menu** button at the top of the window

2 Tap on this button to bookmark the page

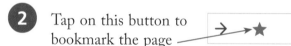

3 Tap on the button in Step 2 again to edit a bookmark. Tap here in the **Folder** box to specify a folder into which you want to save a bookmark

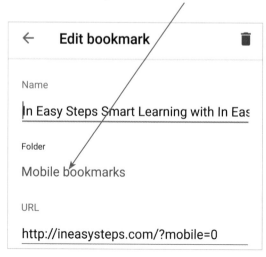

4 Tap on a folder to select it, or tap on the **New folder...** button to create a new folder to use

5 Give the folder a name and tap on the tick symbol to create the folder. Then,
click the arrow button to save and return to the page

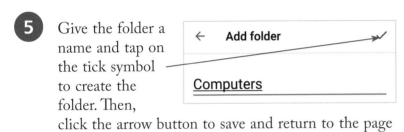

Viewing bookmarks

To view pages that have been bookmarked:

1 To view bookmarks, tap on the **Menu** button and tap on the **Bookmarks** option

2 If folders have been created, tap on one to view its contents

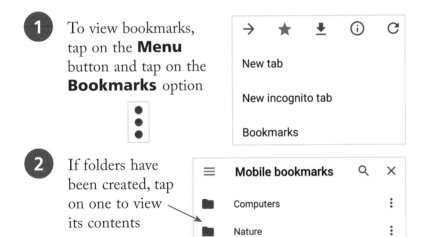

3 Tap on a bookmarked page to open the page in the Chrome browser

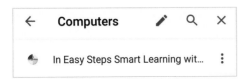

The **Menu** button can also be used to open a new tab. See page 179 for more details about using tabs.

Links and Images

Links and images are both essential items on websites; links provide the functionality for moving between pages and sites, while images provide the all-important graphical element. To work with these:

1 Tap and hold on a link to access its options (tap once on a link to go directly to the linked page). The options include opening the link in a new tab, opening it in a new tab that does not get recorded by the browser's history (**Open in incognito tab**), copying the web address or link text so that it can be shared with someone or pasted into a document, and downloading the link so that it can be viewed offline

> http://ineasysteps.com/products-page/all_books/photoshop-elements-15-tips-tricks-shortcuts-easy-steps/
>
> Open in new tab
>
> Open in incognito tab
>
> Copy link address
>
> Copy link text
>
> Download link

2 Tap and hold on an image to access its options. The options include downloading it, viewing it on its own (**Open image in new tab**), searching Google for the image, or sharing the image

> Download image
>
> Open image in new tab
>
> Search Google for this image
>
> Share image

Using Tabs

Tabs are a common feature on web browsers and allow you to open numerous pages within the same browser window. To do this on an Android phone:

1 Tap on this button at the top right-hand corner of the browser window to view current tabs

Don't forget

The button in Step 1 displays the number of tabs currently open within the Chrome browser.

2 Tap on this button to add a new tab

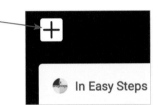

3 Open a new page from the **Search or type URL** box, or any bookmarked pages that are displayed

4 Tap on the button in Step 1 to view all tabs. Tap on a tabbed page to open it. Press and hold on the top of a page and drag it into a different position on the tabs screen

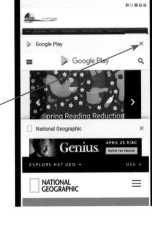

Hot tip

If there are a lot of tabs open, swipe up and down in the tabs window to view them.

5 Tap on the cross on a tab to close it

Being Incognito

If you do not want a record to be kept of the web pages that you have visited, most browsers have a function where you can view pages "in private" so that the details are not stored by the browser. In Chrome, this is performed with the Incognito function:

Don't forget

If the Incognito option is used, web pages will not be stored in the browser history or the search history.

1 Tap on the **Menu** button and tap on the **New incognito tab** option

New tab

New incognito tab

2 The incognito page opens in a new tab, but any other open tabs are not visible (unless they are incognito too). Open a web page in the same way as for a standard tab

Beware

If children are using your phone, you may not know what they are looking at on the web if they use the Incognito option.

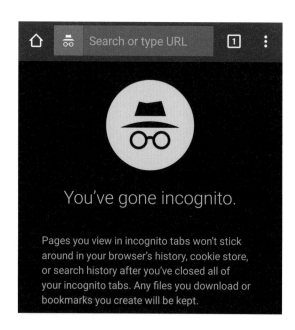

Search or type URL

You've gone incognito.

Pages you view in incognito tabs won't stick around in your browser's history, cookie store, or search history after you've closed all of your incognito tabs. Any files you download or bookmarks you create will be kept.

3 Incognito pages are denoted by this icon at the top left-hand corner of the browser

Browser Settings

Mobile browsers have the usual range of settings that can be accessed from the **Menu** button.

1 Tap on the **Menu** button and tap on the **Settings** option

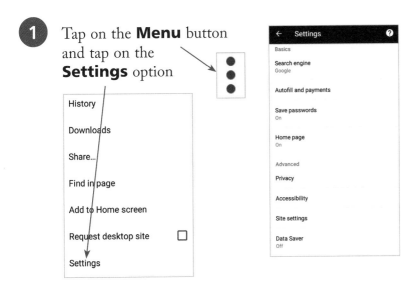

Some of the Settings include:

- **Search engine**. This can be used to set a default search engine for the browser.

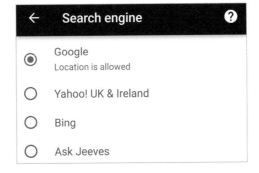

- **Auto-fill forms**. Use this to make selections for how online forms are dealt with by the browser.

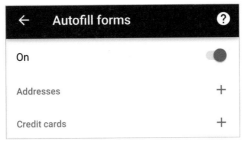

Beware

If other people are going to be using your account on your phone, do not turn on auto-fill options for credit or debit cards.

...cont'd

- Under the **Advanced** heading, tap on the **Privacy** option to specify how your browsing data is used.

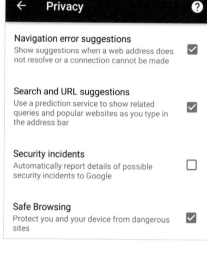

- Under the **Advanced** heading, tap on the **Accessibility** option to specify the text size for viewing web pages.

A cookie is a small piece of data that is stored by the browser, containing information about websites that have been visited.

- Under the **Advanced** heading, tap on the **Site settings** option. Select each option in turn, and then check on or off the options for cookies, JavaScript (which is required to give you full functionality of most websites) and pop-up menus. Tap on the **Location** option to specify whether other websites can use your current location, and the **All sites** option to view settings for individual websites.

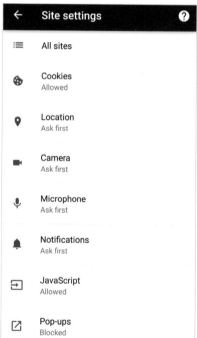

- Under the **Advanced** heading, tap on the **Data Saver** option to specify how web pages are pre-loaded.

12 Staying Secure

This chapter looks at security issues.

184 Security Issues

185 About Antivirus Apps

186 Locating Your Phone

Security Issues

Security is a significant issue for all forms of computing and this is no different for Android phone users. Three of the main areas of concern are:

- **Getting viruses from apps**. Android apps can contain viruses like any other computer programs, but there are antivirus apps that can be used to try to detect viruses. Unlike programs on computers or laptops with file management systems, apps on a phone tend to be 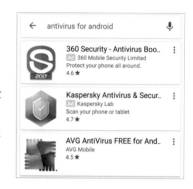 more self-contained and do not interact with the rest of the system. This means that if they do contain viruses it is less likely that they will infect the whole phone.

- **Losing your phone or having it stolen**. If your phone is lost or stolen you will want to try to get it back and also lock it remotely so that no-one else can gain access to your data and content. The Google Account web page has an option for finding a lost phone (see page 186), and some antivirus apps also have this option.

- **Restricting access for children**. If you have young children or grandchildren who are using your phone, you will want to know what they are using it for. This is particularly important for the web, social media sites, video sharing sites and 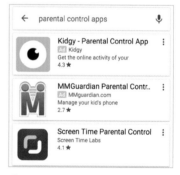 messaging sites where there is the potential to interact with other people. There is also a range of parental control apps that can be downloaded from the Play Store. These can be used to limit access to certain types of apps or content.

About Antivirus Apps

Android phones are certainly not immune from viruses and malware, and the FBI's Internet Crime Complaint Center (IC3) has even published advice and information about malicious software aimed at Android users. Some general precautions that can be taken to protect your phone are:

- Use an antivirus app on your phone. There are several of these, and they can scan your phone for any existing viruses and also check new apps and email attachments for potential problems.

- Apps that are provided in the Play Store are checked for viruses before they are published, but if you are in any doubt about an app, research it online before you download it. If you do an online search for the app, any issues related to it should be available.

- Do not download any email attachments if you are not sure of their authenticity. If you do not know the person who has sent the email then delete it.

Functionality of antivirus apps

There are several antivirus apps available in the Play Store. Search for **android antivirus apps** (or similar) to view the apps. Most security apps have a similar range of features:

- **Scanning** for viruses and malicious software (malware).

- **Online protection** against malicious software on websites.

- **Anti-theft protection.** This can be used to lock your phone, locate it through location services, wipe its contents if they are particularly sensitive, and instruct it to let out an alert sound.

For some of the functions of antivirus and security apps a sign-in is required.

A lot of antivirus and security apps are free, but there is usually a Pro or Premium version that has to be paid for. It is worth downloading several of the free versions of antivirus apps, to see how you like them and to try out the different functions that they have.

Some antivirus apps also have an option for backing up items such as your contacts, which can then be restored to your phone or another device if they are deleted or corrupted at all.

Locating Your Phone

If you lose your phone or it is stolen, you can try to find its location via the Google Account website.

A lost phone has to be turned on and Location enabled in **Settings** > **Network connections** for it to be located via the Google Account website.

1 Log in to your online Google Account at: **myaccount.google.com/**

2 Click on the **Get started** button under the **Find your phone** heading (at this point you will have to sign in to your Google Account again, which is a security feature for locating your phone)

3 Click on the device to locate

Samsung Galaxy S5

4 The options for accessing the lost phone are listed. These include locating it, locking it, calling it, signing out from it, and getting in touch with your phone carrier. Click on the **Locate** button to locate the phone using Android Device Manager

5 The device is shown on a map. Use these buttons to, from left to right, ring the phone, lock it or erase the data on it

Symbols

3G networks	16
3x4 keyboard	110-111
In portrait mode	110
4G networks	16

A

Accented letters.	
See Keyboard: Accented letters	
Accessibility	47-50
Explore by Touch	48
Magnification gestures	48
Adding contacts	80-81
From a call	82
From a text	83
Address book (Contacts app)	124
Airplane mode	14
All Apps button	52
Android	
Characteristics	8
Checking version	9
Overview	8
Updating	10
Version names	9
Viewing version	10
Anti-theft apps	185
Antivirus apps	185
Apps	
Adding to the Home screen	54
Closing	53
Downloading	138-139
Finding	136-137
Force stopping	144
Information	144
In the Play Store	134-135
Moving	55
New	134
Uninstalling	140

Updating	142-143
Updating automatically	142
Updating manually	143
Using	24

B

Back button	53
Background	
Changing	58
Backing up	19, 43
Battery usage	
Saving	40
Bluetooth	
For calls	91
Sharing photos	172
Bookmarks.	
See Websites: Bookmarking pages	
Books.	See Ebooks
Navigation	53

C

Call logs	82
Calls	
Accepting	90
Bluetooth	91
End call	92
Making	88-89
Making a quick call	89
Receiving	90-92
Rejecting	90
Rejecting with a text message	90
Speaker	91
Camera	162
Controls	162
For video calls	88
Modes	163
Using	162-163

Caps Lock	98
Cellular networks	16
Chrome browser	175
Clock	124
Connecting to the Internet	
With Wi-Fi	17
Contacts	
Adding	80-81
Adding ringtones	87
Copying from Phone to SIM	84-85
Editing	86-87
Importing from SIM card	85
Saving from a call	82
Saving from texts	83
Searching for	89
Transferring from phone to SIM	84
Contacts app	80
Cookies	182

E

Ebooks	
Around	160
Deleting	160
Obtaining	158
Reading settings	160
Table of Contents	160
Email.	*See also* Gmail
Attachment security	185
Setting up	118-119
Emojis	112-113
Quick insert	112
Searching for	113

F

Facebook	131
Favorites	56
Favorites Tray	52, 56
FBI Internet Crime Complaint Center	185
Finding items	68-69
Find your phone	186

Fingerprint sensor	15
Fit app	132
Folders	
Adding to the Favorites Tray	59
Creating	59
Font size	47

G

Games	133
Gboard.	*See also* Keyboard
Google search button	102
Numbers bar	98
Settings	103
Shortcuts bar	102-103
Gift cards	
Redeeming	135
Glide typing	115
Gmail	18
Accessing	118
Accessing emails	120
Accessing mailboxes	120
Adding accounts	118-119
Adding attachments	121
Creating email	121
Formatting text	121
Setting up	118-119
Using	120-121
Google	10, 18, 68
Search options	68-69
Google+	131
Google Account	
About	18
From the Settings app	19
Obtaining	20-21
Payment	18
Google Assistant	71-72
When traveling	72
Google Feeds	
About	74
Accessing	75
Cards	74
Customizing	77
Gmail cards	75

Google Maps 126, 128-129
Google Now. *See* Google Feeds
Google Pixel 10, 28
Google Play
   Music 147
   Using 146
Google Search box 52, 68, 76
Google Translate 103

H

Hands-free 122
Haptic feedback 38
Headphone jack 15
Headphones 151
Hearing settings 49
Health and fitness 132
Home button 53
Home screen 52
   Accessing Quick Settings 52
   All Apps button 52
   Favorites Tray 52
   Google Search box 52
   Main area 52
   Moving between 53
   Notifications Bar 52
   Viewing 52
HTC 31
Huawei 32

I

IC3. *See* FBI Internet Crime Complaint Center
Instagram 131
Internet messaging 108

J

Jelly Bean 10

K

Keyboard
   About 98-99
   Accented letters 104
   Auto capitalization 101
   Auto-correction 101
   Back delete 99, 105
   Double-space period 101
   Dual functions 104
   Go button 99
   Hiding 99
   Next-word suggestions 101, 105
   Number pad 99
   Predictive text 100
   Preferences 100
   Send button 99
   Settings 100-101
   Shortcuts 104
   Show emoji suggestions 101
   Show suggestions 101, 105
   Spacebar shortcut 104
   Suggest contact names 101
   Symbols 99
   Viewing 98
Keyboards 96
   Selecting 97
Kindle 158
KitKat 10

L

Landscape mode 62
Lenovo 33
LG 34
Linux 8
Locating your phone 186
Locking
   Fingerprint 66
   Password 66-67
   Pattern 66-67

PIN   66-67
    Your phone   66-67
Lollipop   10
Losing your phone   185-186

M

macOS   8
Malware   185
Managing apps   24
Maps   128-129
    Getting directions   129
    Viewing locations   128
Marshmallow   9, 10
Memo app   130
Memos   130
Messages app   108
Messaging apps   86
Microphone
    Accessing   122
microSD cards   15
Micro USB port   15
Motorola   30
Movies   156-157
Multiple windows   63-65
    Editing windows   65
Music
    Artwork   149
    Clear queue   153
    Downloading from Play Store   148-149
    Managing   153
    On Android   147
    Pinning   154-155
    Playing   150-152
        Controls   152
    Sample content   148

N

Navigation   53
Near Field Communication (NFC)   42

Notes   130
Notifications   60-61
    Allowing   61
    Clearing   60
    Quick settings   13
    Replying to   12
    Settings   60-61
    Viewing full details   60
Notification panel   60
Notifications bar   52, 60
Nougat   12-13

O

OK Google   73
    Training for your voice   73
Online protection   185
On/Off button   14
    For sleeping a phone   14
Organizing apps   59
Overlays   11

P

Payment
    Through a Google Account   18
Photos
    Adding   164-165
    Cropping   171
    Editing   170-171
    From email   165
    Obtaining   164
    Sharing   172
    Transferring   164
    Viewing   166-168
Photos app   164-168
    Adding folders   169
    For editing photos   170-171
    For viewing photos   166-168
Pinterest   131
Play Books   18, 158-159

Play Movies & TV   18, 156-157
Play Music
    Subscription service   147
Play Music app
    Downloading music   148-149
    Managing music   153
    Pinning music   154-155
    Playing Music   150-152
Play Newsstand   18
Play Store   18, 24, 54
    Categories   137
    Downloading apps   138-139
    Finding apps   136-137
    Gift cards   135
    Navigating around   134-135
Portrait mode   62
Power off   14

Q

Quick contact messaging   109
Quick Settings   45-46, 52
    Editing   46
Quick Switch   12
QWERTY keyboard   99

R

RAM   26
Receiving calls   90-92
Recent Items button   53
Rejecting calls   90
Restart   14
Restricting access
    For children   184
Ringtones   93-94
    Downloading   94
    Using your own music   93
Rotating the screen   62
Routers for Wi-Fi access   17

S

Samsung   26-27
Screen lock   66-67
Screen rotation   62
Searching   68-70
    Voice search   69-70
Security issues   184
Selfies   15, 162
Settings
    Accessing   36
    Accessing from Quick Settings   36
    Applications   44
    Connect and share   42
    Network connections   37
    Personalization   39
    Sound and display   38
    System   40-41
    User and backup   43
Setting up   17-18
    Apps & data   17
    Google Account   17
    Google Feeds   17
    Google services   17
    Language   17
    Wi-Fi   17
SIM cards   16
SIM tray   16
Sleep mode   14
Smileys   113
Snapchat   131
Social media   131
    Facebook   131
    Instagram   131
    Pinterest   131
    Snapchat   131
    Twitter   131
Sony   29
Streaming   150
Swipe
    To unlock   66
Swiping
    On a web page   175

T

TalkBack	47-48
Text	
Adding	105
Copy and paste	106
Selecting	106
Texting	
Attachments	114
Background	116
Bubbles	116
Changing the skin	116-117
Contacts	108-109
Deleting conversation threads	108
Large attachments	114
Using the 3x4 keyboard	110-111
Touchscreen	
Pressing	23
Protecting from moisture	22
Swiping	23
Tapping	23
Using	22-23
TouchWiz interface	26
Turning off	14
Turning on	14, 17
TV shows	156-157
Twitter	131

U

USB port	
For attaching to a computer	15
For charging	15

V

Video calls	15, 88
Videos	
Personal	
Adding	164

Viruses	184
Vision settings	47-48
Voice typing	103
Volume button	14

W

Wake up	
From sleep	14
Wallpaper	58
Wallpaper apps	
Downloading	58
Web browsers	
Android	174
Web pages	
Navigating around	175
Websites	
Bookmarking pages	176-177
Browser settings	181-182
Images	178
Incognito browsing	180
Links	178
Mobile versions	174
Opening pages	175
Private browsing	180
Tabs	179
WhatsApp	86
Widgets	
Adding	57
Wi-Fi hotspots	37

Y

YouTube	127, 131

Z

Zooming in and out	
On web pages	175